The Annual Report of the Council of Inspectors General on Financial Oversight

JULY 2012

Message from the Chair

During the last year, the Council of Inspectors General on Financial Oversight (CIGFO), which includes Inspectors General of nine major financial regulators, established its first working group, monitored Financial Stability Oversight Council (FSOC) activities and held meetings to discuss and share information on financial oversight at each CIGFO member agency.

At the same time FSOC ruled on how it would designate nonbank firms for Federal Reserve supervision, and continued establishing operations in anticipation of fully utilizing its statutory powers to designate both nonbank financial firms and financial market utilities as systemically important to U.S. financial stability. FSOC used its new designation authorities on May 22, 2012 when it tentatively approved for designation certain financial market utilities for additional supervision.

CIGFO deliberations led to the establishment, on December 8, 2011, of a working group on the subject of FSOC controls over non-public information, which focused on information security requirements as they pertain to the safeguarding of information collected by, and exchanged with, FSOC federal agency members.

Led by Jon Rymer, Inspector General, Federal Deposit Insurance Corporation, the working group was comprised of the Offices of Inspectors General for the following agencies:

Board of Governors of the Federal Reserve System

U.S. Commodity Futures Trading Commission

Federal Deposit Insurance Corporation

Federal Housing Finance Agency

National Credit Union Administration

U.S. Securities and Exchange Commission

U.S. Department of the Treasury

On June 26, 2012, the working group issued its report entitled, *Audit of the Financial Stability Oversight Council's Controls over Non-public Information.* This audit included a review of procedures in place at FSOC member agencies, the Office of Financial Research, and the Federal Insurance Office.

The report points out that FSOC understands that its ability to safely share information among its members is critical and, to protect this information from unauthorized disclosure, FSOC members have entered into a memorandum of understanding. The working group report highlights several areas for FSOC's consideration as it moves forward. Specifically, CIGFO encourages FSOC to continue its ongoing efforts to protect non-public information, further examine the issues raised in our report with respect to commonalities and differences of FSOC member agencies, and prepare for possible security upgrades for information that may need to be exchanged as economic conditions change and new threats to the stability of the U.S. financial system emerge. Our report underscores the importance of acting in a timely manner.

In the future, CIGFO will continue reviewing FSOC's compliance with the Dodd-FrankAct to ensure continued rigorous oversight of the U.S. financial system.

Sincerely,

Eric M. Thorson
Chair,Council of Inspectors General
on Financial Oversight
Inspector General, Department of the Treasury

Table of Contents

The Council of Inspectors General on Financial Oversight

The Council of Inspectors General on Financial Oversight (CIGFO), which was established by the Dodd-Frank Wall Street Reform and Consumer Protection Act (Dodd-Frank), meets on a quarterly basis to facilitate the sharing of information among Inspectors General and to discuss the ongoing work of each Inspector General who is a member of the Council, with a focus on concerns that may apply to the broader financial sector and ways to improve financial oversight. CIGFO also publishes an Annual Report.

In summary during this past year CIGFO members discussed the newly published Commodity Futures Trading Commission (CFTC)/Securities Exchange Commission (SEC) regulation requiring investment advisors to private funds to periodically report data to the SEC for use by FSOC, the newly published FSOC rules for designating nonbank financial companies for additional supervision, Board of Governors of the Federal Reserve Board System (FRB) stress tests, and Office of Financial Research activities.

Throughout the year, each CIGFO member conducted oversight supporting the stability, integrity, and efficiency of the nation's financial system. This was done through evaluations of the transfer of the former Office of Thrift Supervision functions to other banking regulators, audits of the implementation of Dodd-Frank, reviews of failed banks, investigations of mortgage fraud, as well as audits of the supervision over the Government-Sponsored Enterprises.

The general belief of each Inspector General that is a member of CIGFO is that significant steps have been taken to implement Dodd Frank, and other regulations, yet more needs to be done to ensure financial sector stability. In fact, the individual OIG reports contained within this report provide recommendations that, if adopted, would improve the management and monitoring of the financial system. Below are some examples of Inspectors General recommendations:

- Federal Housing Finance Agency (FHFA) IG recommends that FHFA negotiate with Treasury and the Enterprises to develop a dispute resolution process.

- Inspectors General of the FDIC, FRB, and Treasury recommend that each agency review the matters for consideration presented in their Prompt Regulatory Action (PRA) report and work through FSOC to determine whether the Prompt Regulatory Action legislation or implementing regulations should be modified.

- Federal Deposit Insurance Corporation (FDIC) IG recommends that controls for monitoring risk sharing agreements be improved.

CIGFO also established its first working group on December 8, 2011. This working group was tasked with evaluating FSOC controls over non-public information and the manner in which FSOC as a whole safeguards information from unauthorized disclosure. This group was led by FDIC Inspector General Jon Rymer and comprised of the IGs of the FRB, the CFTC, the FDIC, the FHFA, the National Credit Union Administration (NCUA), SEC, and Treasury.

On June 26, 2012, the working group issued its report entitled, *Audit of the Financial Stability Oversight Council's Controls over Non-public Information*. The report points out that FSOC understands that its ability to safely share information among its members is critical and, to protect this information from unauthorized disclosure, FSOC members have entered into a memorandum of understanding. The report also highlights several areas for FSOC's consideration as it moves forward. Specifically, CIGFO encourages FSOC to continue its ongoing efforts to protect non-public information, further examine the issues raised in the report with respect to commonalities and differences of FSOC member agencies, and prepare for possible security upgrades for information that may need to be exchanged as economic conditions change and new threats to the stability of the U.S. financial system emerge. The report underscores the importance of acting in a timely manner.

Joint CIGFO Member Oversight

Audit of the Financial Stability Oversight Council's Controls over Non-public Information

On December 8, 2011, Jon Rymer, Inspector General, Federal Deposit Insurance Corporation, and Vice Chair, CIGFO, proposed convening a working group to examine FSOC's controls and protocols for ensuring that its non-public information, deliberations, and decisions are properly safeguarded from unauthorized disclosure. The proposal was approved and the CIGFO Working Group was formed.

The CIGFO Working Group identified the controls and protocols in place at each of the FSOC federal agency members to safeguard FSOC information and the manner in which FSOC as a whole safeguards information from unauthorized disclosure. We reported that FSOC understands that its ability to safely share information among its members is critical to its effectiveness. At the time of this review, a limited amount of non-public information had been exchanged among Council members. Joint work among FSOC members to identify and mitigate risks to financial stability had begun, and data sharing will expand as OFR continues to build its capacity. To protect the exchange of information, the Council members entered into a memorandum of understanding governing the treatment of non-public information that relies on each agency to use the controls in place at their respective agencies.

This report in its entirety can be found in Appendix A.

Reviews of the Status of the Transfer of Office of Thrift Supervision Functions

The OIGs of the FRB the FDIC, and the Treasury completed three reviews of the transfer, pursuant to Title III of the Dodd-Frank Act, of the functions, employees, funds, and property of the Office of Thrift Supervision (OTS) to the FRB, the FDIC, and the OCC. In accordance with Title III, the transfer occurred in July 2011.

The reviews are mandated by Section 327 of Title III. In March 2011, the group issued its report on its first joint review determining whether a Joint Implementation Plan (Plan) for the transfer prepared by the FRB, the FDIC, the OCC, and the OTS conformed to relevant Title III provisions. Based on that review, the group concluded that the Plan generally conformed to the relevant provisions of Title III. The group noted, however, that the Plan did not address the prohibition in Title III against the involuntary separation or the involuntary reassignment of a transferred OTS employee outside the employee's locality pay area for 30 months (except under certain circumstances). In response to a recommendation to address this matter, the agencies amended the Plan in April 2011.

After the initial joint review of the Plan, Section 327 requires that every 6 months the Offices of Inspector General of the FRB, the FDIC and the Treasury jointly provide a written report on the status of the implementation of the Plan to the FRB, the FDIC, and the OCC, with a copy to the Congress. The group issued two reports, in September 2011 and March 2011, under this requirement. In those reports, the group concluded that the FRB, the FDIC, the OCC, and the OTS implemented the actions in the Plan that were necessary to transfer OTS functions, employees, and funds to the FRB, the FDIC, and the OCC, as appropriate. The group also concluded that all OTS property was transferred to those three agencies, and procedures and safeguards are in place as outlined in the Plan to ensure transferred employees are not unfairly disadvantaged. However, there are certain other items related to the Plan that are ongoing or are not yet required to be completed as provided in Title III. In accordance with Section 327, the group will continue to monitor the implementation of the Plan until all aspects have been implemented.

Review of Prompt Regulatory Action

The OIGs of the Treasury, the FDIC, and the FRB conducted a review of the (Prompt Regulatory Action (PRA)) provisions of Federal Deposit Insurance Act (FDIA). The PRA provisions include Section 38 Prompt Corrective Action (PCA) and Section 39 (Standards for Safety and Soundness). Sections 38 and 39 were intended to assist in the identification of problem banks and provide tools for regulators to ensure consistent, timely enforcement action designed to minimize losses to the Deposit Insurance Fund .

The work by the group was designed to explore the history and purpose of the PRA provisions, the extent to which the provisions were a factor in the most recent crisis, and other non-capital measures that provide a leading indication of risk that should be considered as part of PRA.

While the joint effort found that PCA was appropriately implemented and helped strengthen oversight to a degree, the group also reported the following:

- Inherent limitations associated with PCA's capital-based framework and the sudden and severe economic decline impacted PCA's effectiveness in resolving the problems of institutions during this crisis.
- Regulators identified deficiencies prior to declines in PCA capital categories.
- Regulators took action to address safety and soundness concerns before undercapitalization but after financial decline occurred.
- Regulators made limited use of Section 39 to address asset quality and management deficiencies.
- Critically undercapitalized institutions were closed promptly, but overall losses were significant.

The group concluded that a key question going forward was how to effectively address safety and soundness concerns prior to financial deterioration to avoid, or at least lessen, significant failures and losses emanating from a future crisis. The group also identified non-capital factors that are leading indicators of potential troubles, such as high-risk business strategies that include for example, aggressive growth, asset concentrations, and dependence on volatile funding sources; risk management weaknesses such as poor underwriting and credit administration practices; and asset quality or earnings deterioration. Using these factors as triggers for mandatory regulatory intervention may strengthen the PRA framework.

To improve the effectiveness of the PRA framework and to meet the Section 38 and Section 39 goals of identifying problems early and minimizing losses to the Deposit Insurance Fund, the OIGs recommended that the FDIC, the FRB, and the OCC review the matters for consideration presented in their report and work through FSOC to determine whether the PRA legislation or regulations should be modified. The specific matters for consideration are (1) developing specific criteria and corresponding enforcement actions for non-capital factors, (2) increasing the minimum PCA capital levels, and (3) continuing to refine the deposit insurance system for banks with assets under $10 billion to assess greater premiums commensurate with risk-taking.

Council of Inspectors General on Financial Oversight Activities

June 2011- June 2012

July 2011

CIGFO met on July 20, 2011, a presentation from the Minnesota Economic Crimes Division on bank fraud, and a presentation from the Treasury Deputy Assistant Secretary, Financial Stability Oversight Council on the FSOC designation process. CIGFO Members unanimously approved the release of a letter from CIGFO to FSOC containing recommendations for change to the proposed rule on designation of certain nonbank firms for heightened supervision.

CIGFO released its first Annual Report on July 21, 2011.

December 2011

On December 8, 2011 CIGFO members unanimously approved the establishment of a working group to evaluate the FSOC's protocols and controls over non-public information. In addition, a presentation and discussion was held on the CFTC/SEC rule requiring investment advisors to private funds to periodically report data to the SEC as it will be used by FSOC to monitor private fund assets. Finally, the CIGFO continued its discussions with FSOC concerning the FSOC's approach to designating nonbank financial companies for supervision by the FRB.

March 2012

At a March 30, 2012 meeting, CIGFO members discussed the results of recent FRB bank stress tests, as well as the progress of the working group to evaluate FSOC controls over non-public information. Discussion also included the FSOC Annual Report issued July 2011, the Office of Financial Research, and a Congressional request to CIGFO .

May 2012

CIGFO members met on May 21 and unanimously approved the final draft of the CIGFO report titled, *Audit of the Financial Stability Oversight Council's Controls over Non-Public Information.* Members also reviewed and discussed recent FSOC and Congressional activities.

June 2012

On June 26, 2012, CIGFO released its report, *Audit of the Financial Stability Oversight Council's Controls over Non-public Information*, and provided copies of it to Congress and FSOC.

Financial Stability Oversight Council Activities

June 2011- June 2012

July 13, 2011

The FSOC convened by teleconference to discuss the 2011 annual report.

July 18, 2011

The FSOC met and approved a report to Congress regarding the importance of maximizing U.S. taxpayer protections and promoting market discipline with respect to the treatment of fully secured creditors in the utilization of the orderly liquidation authority, as well as the rule concerning the criteria, processes, and procedures for the designation of certain financial market utilities (FMUs). The FSOC also approved minutes from prior meetings. Presentations were given to the Council on the 2011 annual report and current macro-economic environment, designation of nonbank financial companies, and enhanced prudential standards.

July 22, 2011

The FSOC approved the 2011 annual report through a notational vote.

August 8, 2011

The FSOC convened by teleconference to discuss market developments in light of increased financial market volatility and risk aversion.

September 15, 2011

The FSOC convened by teleconference to discuss market developments in light of increased market volatility and European market developments.

October 11, 2011

The FSOC met and approved the revised notice of proposed rulemaking and proposed interpretive guidance regarding the designation of nonbank financial companies, its budget for fiscal year 2012, and minutes from prior meetings.   Under section 155 of the Dodd-Frank Act any FSOC expenses are required to be funded by transfers from FRB for the first 2 years after the date of enactment of the law (July 21, 2010). After 2 years the expenses of the Office of Financial Research and FSOC will be funded through assessments on bank holding companies (BHCs) with greater than $50 billion in assets and nonbank financial companies supervised by the FRB. Assessments will be set through regulation by the Treasury Secretary.

Presentations were given to the FSOC regarding the macro-economic environment and Europe, money market fund reform efforts, the 2011 annual report recommendations, and the development of enhanced prudential standards.

October 31, 2011

The FSOC convened by teleconference to discuss developments regarding MF Global.

November 11, 2011

The FSOC convened by teleconference to discuss European market developments.

December 5, 2011

The FSOC met and received presentations on the macro-economic environment and Europe, housing market issues, Dodd-Frank coordination efforts, and the evaluation of FMUs for potential designation. The FSOC also approved minutes from prior meetings.

December 21, 2012

The FSOC convened by teleconference and approved the advancement of certain FMUs from stage 1 to stage 2 of the designation process, Treasury's publication of a notice of proposed rulemaking regarding the assessment schedule to fund the Financial Research Fund, and a report to Congress on prompt corrective action.

February 1, 2012

FSOC met and received presentations on the the macro-economic environment and Europe, money market fund reform efforts, public comments on the notice of proposed rulemaking and proposed interpretive guidance on nonbank financial company designations, Dodd-Frank Act implementation, and the 2012 annual report. The FSOC also approved minutes from prior meetings.

April 3, 2012

The FSOC met and received presentations on macro-economic trends and energy markets, critical infrastructure issues, the Federal Reserve's comprehensive capital analysis and review process, the 2012 annual report, and the FMU designation process. The FSOC also approved the final rule and interpretive guidance on nonbank financial company designations and the final rule implementing the Freedom of Information Act, appointed a Chairperson of the Deputies Committee, and approved minutes from a prior meeting..

May 22, 2012

The FSOC met and received presentations on the macro-economic environment and Europe and recent trading losses at JP Morgan Chase & Co. The FSOC also approved the proposed designation of an initial set FMUs based on stage 2 evaluations, approved hearing procedures relating to proposed designations of nonbank financial companies and FMUs, and approved minutes from a prior meeting.

June 11, 2012

The FSOC met and received presentations on the macro-economic environment and Europe, recent trading losses at JP Morgan Chase & Co, the 2012 annual report, and tri-party repo. The FSOC approved a report to Congress on actions taken in response to the U.S. GAO's report on the NCUA's supervision of corporate credit unions and implementation of prompt corrective action, as well as minutes from a prior meeting.

Individual Reports of Inspectors General

Under the leadership of the Treasury Inspector General, CIGFO leveraged the expertise and experience of its Inspector General members, who bring unique independent perspectives on important issues and provide collective and individual views through joint projects, the efforts of the CIGFO working group and individual audits.

As required by Section 989E of Dodd-Frank, the CIGFO Annual Report must include:

For each inspector general who is a member of the Council of Inspectors General, a section within the exclusive editorial control of such inspector general that highlights the concerns and recommendations of such inspector general in such inspector general's ongoing and completed work, with a focus on issues that may apply to the broader financial sector.

To that end this section includes reports from the following Inspectors General:

- Board of Governors of the Federal Reserve System
- U.S. Commodity Futures Trading Commission
- U.S. Department of Housing and Urban Development
- U.S. Department of the Treasury
- Federal Deposit Insurance Corporation
- Federal Housing Finance Agency
- National Credit Union Administration
- U.S. Securities and Exchange Commission
- Special Inspector General for the Troubled Asset Relief Program

This report highlights the selected efforts of each CIGFO Inspector General as they relate to issues impacting the broader financial sector and financial oversight. The work presented in these individual reports was not conducted under the auspices of CIGFO but, rather, represents completed or ongoing work on issues of mutual interest or concern, as well as important bodies of work specific to each Inspector General's respective agency.

Office of Inspector General
Board of Governors of the Federal Reserve System and Consumer Financial Protection Bureau

I. Background

With the enactment of the Inspector General Act Amendments of 1988, Congress established the Office of Inspector General (OIG) as an independent oversight authority for the Board of Governors of the Federal Reserve System (Board)—the government agency component of the broader Federal Reserve System. In addition, on July 21, 2010, the Dodd-Frank Wall Street Reform and Consumer Protection Act (Dodd-Frank Act) statutorily established the OIG as the independent oversight authority for the Consumer Financial Protection Bureau (CFPB).

Under the authority of the Inspector General Act of 1978, as amended (IG Act), the OIG conducts independent and objective audits, inspections, evaluations, investigations, and other reviews related to the programs and operations of the Board and the CFPB. Through its work, the OIG promotes integrity, economy, efficiency, and effectiveness; helps prevent and detect fraud, waste, and abuse; and strengthens the agencies' accountability to Congress and the public.

In addition to the duties set forth in the IG Act, Congress has mandated additional responsibilities for the OIG. Section 38(k) of the Federal Deposit Insurance Act (FDI Act) requires that the OIG review failed financial institutions supervised by the Board that result in a material loss to the Deposit Insurance Fund (DIF) and produce a report within six months. The Dodd-Frank Act amended section 38(k) of the FDI Act by raising the materiality threshold and requiring the OIG to report on the results of any nonmaterial losses to the DIF that exhibited unusual circumstances warranting an in-depth review.

In addition, section 211(f) of the Dodd-Frank Act requires that the OIG review the Board's supervision of any covered financial company that is placed into receivership. The OIG will produce a report that evaluates the effectiveness of the Board's supervision, identifies any acts or omissions by the Board that contributed to or could have prevented the company's receivership status, and recommends appropriate administrative or legislation action.

Section 11B of the Federal Reserve Act mandates annual independent audits of the financial statements of each Federal Reserve Bank and the Board. Our office oversees the annual financial statement audits of the Board, as well as the Federal Financial Institutions Examination Council (FFIEC). The FFIEC is a formal interagency body empowered to prescribe uniform principles, standards, and report forms for the federal examination of financial institutions by the Board, the Federal Deposit Insurance Corporation, the National Credit Union Administration, the Office of the Comptroller of the Currency, and the CFPB and to make recommendations to promote uniformity in the supervision of financial institutions. In 2006, the State Liaison Committee was added to the FFIEC as a voting member. The State Liaison Committee includes representatives from the Conference of State Bank Supervisors, the American Council of State Savings Supervisors, and the National Association of State Credit Union Supervisors.

With respect to information technology, the Federal Information Security Management Act of 2002 established a legislative mandate to ensure the effectiveness of information security controls over resources that support federal operations and assets. Consistent with the act's requirements, our office performs an annual independent evaluation of the Board's and the CFPB's information security programs and practices, including the effectiveness of security controls and techniques for selected information systems.

II. OIG Reports and Other Products Related to the Broader Financial Sector

In accordance with section 989E(a)(2)(B) of the Dodd-Frank Act, the following highlights the completed and ongoing work of our office, with a focus on issues that may apply to the broader financial sector.

COMPLETED WORK

Audit of the Implementation of the Dodd-Frank Wall Street Reform and Consumer Protection Act

Specific to the Board, our office conducted an *Audit of the Implementation of the Dodd-Frank Wall Street Reform and Consumer Protection Act.* The Dodd-Frank Act was enacted in response to the financial crisis and charged the Board with significant responsibilities, including the development of complex rulemakings, many in conjunction with other federal financial regulatory agencies. We conducted this audit to assess (1) the efficiency and effectiveness of the Board's processes for identifying, tracking, and managing its responsibilities under the act and (2) the Board's progress in implementing key requirements of the act.

Overall, we found that the Board has implemented processes and taken significant steps to meet its Dodd-Frank Act responsibilities. The Board has drawn on expertise and resources from across the Federal Reserve System and has over 300 staff members working on its implementation projects. The Board has established an organizational structure with a senior staff position to coordinate its efforts and has developed and implemented the use of project reporting and tracking tools to facilitate management and oversight. Building on these efforts, the Board has completed studies and rulemakings, issued reports, and reorganized and created offices to meet its Dodd-Frank Act obligations. Board project teams are continuing work on Dodd-Frank Act requirements, many of which require interagency involvement.

Notwithstanding this progress, we identified several areas for the Board's continued management attention and monitoring, including (1) managing the overall workload volume and complexity; (2) collaborating and coordinating actions with other financial regulatory agencies that share responsibilities for a number of rules, studies, and other Dodd-Frank Act provisions; (3) obtaining and analyzing voluminous public comments on rulemakings; (4) meeting statutory deadlines; and (5) establishing an organizational structure and recruiting and integrating new staff. In addition to these challenges, we identified opportunities to improve the use of the Board's project reporting and tracking tool.

We noted that some of these challenges adversely affected project completion early in the Board's implementation process. Of the 13 projects with statutory deadlines that fell within the period of our fieldwork, 6 missed their deadlines. Two of these 6 projects stem from a single proposed rulemaking that generated over 11,000 comments. The other 4 projects were delayed due to interagency operational challenges, including one project that the Board approved about one week prior to its deadline. While these projects represent a small percentage of the Board's overall Dodd-Frank Act implementation responsibilities through 2013, they reflect the challenges it faces in its ongoing implementation efforts.

As the bulk of the Board's Dodd-Frank Act work lies ahead, leveraging lessons learned from early implementation challenges can help guide the Board to efficiently and effectively carry out its Dodd-Frank Act requirements going forward. We recommended that the Dodd-Frank Special Advisor to the Board for Regulatory Reform Implementation (1) develop and issue appropriate guidance on the project reporting and tracking tool usage relating to team leader color assessments and the management of projects that have not been completed by their statutory deadlines, and (2) instruct team leaders and project coordinators to evaluate and revise their project information as necessary.

Audit of the Board's Progress in Developing Enhanced Prudential Standards

Our office conducted an *Audit of the Board's Progress in Developing Enhanced Prudential Standards.* Section 165 of the Dodd-Frank Act requires the Board to establish enhanced prudential standards for bank holding companies (BHCs) with total consolidated assets equal to or greater than $50 billion (referred to as "large BHCs") and nonbank financial companies that are determined by the Financial Stability Oversight Council (FSOC) to pose a risk to financial stability. Specifically, section 165 of the Dodd-Frank Act requires that the Board's enhanced prudential standards include (1) risk-based capital requirements and leverage limits, (2) liquidity requirements, (3) overall risk management requirements, (4) resolution plan and credit exposure report requirements, and (5) concentration limits. In addition, the Dodd-Frank Act authorizes but does not require the Board to establish requirements related to contingent capital, enhanced public disclosures, short-term debt limits, and other prudential standards that the Board, either on its own or at the recommendation of FSOC, determines appropriate.

Our audit objective was to assess the Board's Division of Banking Supervision and Regulation's (BS&R's) approach and activities to comply with the Dodd-Frank Act requirements related to developing enhanced prudential standards for large BHCs, including prudential standards that would apply to any nonbank financial company determined by the FSOC to be systemically important. The scope of our work focused on BS&R's progress toward enhancing prudential standards for large BHCs that are currently supervised by one of three BS&R sections: Large Institution Supervision Coordinating Committee, Large Banking Organizations, and International Banking Organizations.

Overall, we found that BS&R had taken a proactive approach to enhancing its supervision of large BHCs, including initiating actions prior to the enactment of the Dodd-Frank Act. BS&R has reorganized its sections to accommodate a new framework for supervision of large BHCs and has taken actions to enhance the supervision of large BHCs to meet the related requirements of the Dodd-Frank Act. As BS&R continues to enhance its supervisory approach, we issued a management letter to BS&R that provided two suggestions for management's consideration that we believe would further strengthen BS&R's efforts to supervise large BHCs and meet related Dodd-Frank Act requirements. First, we suggested that the Large Institution Supervision Coordinating Committee define and document roles and responsibilities for its subgroups involved in large BHC supervision and for coordination with other Board offices, to ensure a clear understanding of each office's purposes and functions. Second, we suggested that BS&R finalize the process for distributing and maintaining a complete list of large BHCs, including BHCs that may fluctuate above or below the $50 billion threshold in asset size, to effectively and timely supervise large BHCs under enhanced prudential standards.

Review of CFPB Implementation Planning Activities

Our office and the Department of the Treasury (Treasury) OIG jointly issued a report on the CFPB's implementation planning activities related to standing up the agency. The review's objective to assess the CFPB's efforts to (1) identify mission-critical activities and legislative mandates, (2) develop and execute a comprehensive implementation plan and timeline for mission-critical activities and legislative mandates, and (3) communicate its implementation plan and timeline to certain key stakeholders.

Our review found that the CFPB identified and documented implementation activities critical to standing up the agency's functions and necessary to address certain Dodd-Frank Act requirements. Further, at the time of our review the CFPB had developed and was implementing appropriate plans to support ongoing operations as well as the July 21, 2011, transfer of employees and functions. We reported the status of the CFPB's implementation progress for certain activities as follows:

- As of June 17, 2011, 19 of the CFPB's 35 assistant director or equivalent positions had been filled. According to the CFPB, the agency also had hired a Regional Director for its San Francisco office and was in the process of recruiting leaders for its Washington, DC; Chicago; and New York offices.

- As of June 30, 2011, the CFPB offered transfers to 349 employees from other federal regulatory agencies. As of that date, 172 employees had accepted the CFPB's transfer offers, and CFPB officials were awaiting additional responses.

- On February 13, 2011, the CFPB developed an interim pay structure to implement a payroll system. On May 8, 2011, the agency refined its pay structure, which comprises 9 pay bands consisting of 18 pay ranges.

- According to CFPB documents, the agency plans to continue using Treasury's Bureau of the Public Debt Administrative Resource Center for its financial management. The CFPB also plans to continue relying on Treasury's infrastructure for its general support systems, such as e-mail. Contractors provide additional information technology support.

- According to CFPB officials, starting on July 21, 2011, the CFPB expected to take website inquiries and phone calls from consumers, initiate the complaint inquiry process, and begin case management to track complaints. However, the agency planned to initially only process complaints related to credit cards. According to a CFPB timeline, the agency planned to process complaints concerning other consumer financial products over the course of the next year.

We also reported that the CFPB communicated its planning and implementation of standup activities to internal stakeholders and provided information to other consumer regulatory agencies regarding its transfer planning. Nevertheless, we concluded that CFPB's operational success will depend, in part, on its ability to effectively execute its plans.

Summary Analysis of Failed Bank Reviews

This report analyzed failed state member bank reports that the OIG issued between June 29, 2009, and June 30, 2011, to determine the common characteristics, circumstances, and emerging themes related to (1) the cause of the bank failures and (2) Federal Reserve supervision of the failed institutions. Our analysis yielded a series of common observations. We also conducted supplemental research and analysis to understand why certain institutions withstood the financial crisis better than others.

With respect to the cause of the state member bank failures, the majority of the analyzed reports cited common themes. In addition to the economic decline that triggered asset quality deterioration and significant losses at each of the failed banks, the common themes included (1) management's robust growth objectives and strategic choices that proved to be poor decisions; (2) rapid loan portfolio growth that exceeded the bank's risk management capabilities and/or internal controls; (3) asset concentrations that were tied to commercial real estate (CRE) or construction, land, and land development (CLD) loans, which increased the bank's vulnerability to changes in the marketplace and compounded the risks inherent in individual loans; and (4) management's failure to have sufficient capital to cushion mounting losses. Additionally, the reports revealed certain practices that contributed to specific failures, such as risky funding strategies and incentive compensation programs that inappropriately encouraged risk-taking.

With respect to the supervision of the failed state member banks, many of the analyzed reports noted that examiners identified key safety and soundness risks, but did not take sufficient supervisory action in a timely manner to compel the boards of directors and management to mitigate those risks. In many instances, examiners eventually concluded that supervisory actions were necessary, but those conclusions came too late to reverse the banks' deteriorating condition.

In our supplemental research and analysis that compared failed banks to those that withstood the financial crisis, we found that lower CRE and CLD concentration levels, strong capital positions, and minimal dependence on non-core funding were key differentiating characteristics of banks that withstood the crisis. Our research also revealed a correlation during the recent financial crisis between high CLD concentration levels and the likelihood of failure during the recent financial crisis.

Based on our mandate to assess the bank failures to determine how losses to the DIF might be avoided in the future and our assessment of the emerging themes from the failures we reviewed, we provided the Director of BS&R with a variety of recommendations and suggestions.

Review of Reserve Bank Operations and Payment Systems' Oversight of the Next Generation $100 Note

We reviewed the Board's Division of Reserve Bank Operations and Payment Systems' (RBOPS's) oversight of the next generation (NXG) $100 note. The Board is the sole issuer of U.S. currency, and RBOPS (on behalf of the Board) is responsible for ensuring the high quality of the Federal Reserve notes that are printed by Treasury's Bureau of Engraving and Printing (BEP). The NXG $100 note is the final denomination to be redesigned in the NXG currency redesign project, which began in 2000. The NXG $100 note includes the most complex anti-counterfeiting security features ever incorporated into U.S. currency.

We began this review as a result of the Board's October 1, 2010, press release announcing that it would delay issuing the NXG $100 note due to the increasing incidence of currency paper creasing during the printing process. Our review objectives were to (1) assess RBOPS' oversight of the design and production of the NXG $100 notes; (2) review the actions RBOPS was taking to address the current printing problems, which include contracting for an independent technical review, and the actions RBOPS is taking to enhance controls to minimize the likelihood of future printing problems; and (3) assess plans for the disposition of NXG $100 notes that have already been printed.

Our analysis determined that actions taken by RBOPS appropriately addressed the identified printing issues and enhanced controls to minimize the likelihood of future printing problems. In addition, we determined that RBOPS staff was participating in the assessment of plans for the disposition of the more than 1.4 billion NXG $100 notes that had been printed. We identified three areas, however, in which RBOPS could strengthen oversight of the Federal Reserve note design and quality control production process:

- RBOPS staff should comply with requirements in a memorandum of understanding (MOU) that details the authorities, responsibilities, and understandings between RBOPS and the BEP, to include agreeing on a limited initial production quantity of newly designed currency.

- The Interagency Currency Design workgroup, which provides technical guidance on currency design and other subjects that affect U.S. currency, should operate under an executed charter.

- The current MOU between the Board and the BEP should be updated and expanded to incorporate the increased complexity of note design, quality control, and production.

Our report contained recommendations to address the absence of (1) an approved and signed Interagency Currency Design workgroup charter, and (2) an updated MOU that incorporates increased design complexities. We did not make a recommendation regarding compliance with requirements in the MOU because the Board entered into an NXG $100 note production validation agreement for the NXG $100 note in September 2011 to ensure that all technical problems are identified and resolved prior to restarting full production.

ONGOING WORK

Audit of the Board's Actions to Analyze Mortgage Foreclosure Processing Risks

Given the public attention on foreclosures, the broad requirements of the Dodd-Frank Act, and the Board's responsibilities as a member of FSOC, we are conducting an audit of the Board's actions to analyze potential risks related to mortgage foreclosures. Our audit objective is to assess the Board's activities in response to potential risks related to mortgage foreclosures.

Review of the Unauthorized Disclosure of a "Confidential Staff Draft" of the Volcker Rule Notice of Proposed Rulemaking

On October 11, 2011, the Board, the FDIC, and the OCC issued press releases requesting public comment on a notice of proposed rulemaking implementing the requirements of section 619 of the Dodd-Frank Act. Section 619, which amends the Bank Holding Company Act of 1956 (12 U.S.C. § 1841 et seq.), contains two key prohibitions on the activities of insured depository institutions, BHCs, and their subsidiaries or affiliates. These two prohibitions are commonly referred to as the "Volcker Rule." The notice of proposed rulemaking to implement the Volcker Rule (referred to hereafter as the NPRM) has attracted considerable attention because the two prohibitions require adjustments to the business models of large, complex banking organizations.

Section 619 required the Board, the Federal Deposit Insurance Corporation (FDIC), the Office of the Comptroller of the Currency (OCC), the Securities and Exchange Commission, and the Commodity Futures Trading Commission (collectively, the agencies) to jointly adopt rules to implement its provisions. As part of this joint rulemaking process, Board employees involved in the rulemaking distributed several versions of the NPRM to the agencies for deliberation, including a "confidential staff draft" dated September 30, 2011. On October 5, 2011, *American Banker*, a banking and financial services media outlet, published this nonpublic, confidential staff draft of the NPRM on its website. The objective of this review is to evaluate whether Board and/or Federal Reserve Bank of New York staff had knowledge of, or played a role in, the unauthorized disclosure of the confidential staff draft of the NPRM and to assess the Board's information-sharing practices for rulemaking activities.

Congressional Request Regarding the Examination Process for Small Community Banks

We received a letter from the Chairman of the Senate Committee on Banking, Housing, and Urban Affairs requesting that we audit the Board's examination process for small community banks. Based on the Chairman's request, we plan to review (1) the Board's examination timelines and how the Board ensures consistency in the administration of examinations throughout the Federal Reserve System, (2) the ability of Board-regulated institutions to question examination results through the Board's Ombudsman program or another appeals process, and (3) the frequency and results of examination appeals.

Office of Inspector General
Commodity Futures Trading Commission

Background

The CFTC OIG was created in 1989 in accordance with the 1988 amendments to the Inspector General Act of 1978 (P.L. 95-452). OIG was established as an independent unit to:

- promote economy, efficiency and effectiveness in the administration of CFTC programs and operations and detect and prevent fraud, waste and abuse in such programs and operations;

- conduct and supervise audits and, where necessary, investigations relating to the administration of CFTC programs and operations;

- review existing and proposed legislation, regulations and exchange rules and make recommendations concerning their impact on the economy and efficiency of CFTC programs and operations or the prevention and detection of fraud and abuse;

- recommend policies for, and conduct, supervise, or coordinate other activities carried out or financed by such establishment for the purpose of promoting economy and efficiency in the administration of, or preventing and detecting fraud and abuse in, its programs and operations;

- and keep the Commission and Congress fully informed about any problems or deficiencies in the administration of CFTC programs and operations and provide recommendations for correction of these problems or deficiencies.

CFTC OIG operates independently of the Agency and has not experienced any interference from the CFTC Chairman in connection with the conduct of any investigation, inspection, evaluation, review, or audit, and our investigations have been pursued regardless of the rank or party affiliation of the target.

Role in Financial Oversight

The CFTC OIG has no direct statutory duties related to oversight of the futures, swaps and derivatives markets; rather, the CFTC OIG acts as an independent Office within the CFTC that conducts investigations, reviews, inspections, and other activities designed to identify fraud, waste, and abuse in connection with CFTC programs and operations, and makes recommendations and referrals as appropriate. The CFTC's yearly financial statement and Customer Protection Fund audits are conducted by an independent public accounting firm, with OIG oversight.

Recent, Current or Ongoing Work in Financial Oversight

1. *Audit of CFTC Controls and Protocols over Sensitive Information Collected and Exchanged with the Financial Stability Oversight Council*

The CFTC is one of nine federal financial agency member of FSOC. In February 2012, each FSOC member's Office of the Inspector General launched an audit at their respective agency with the objective to acquire, evaluate, and report on their respective agency's policies and procedures for managing and protecting FSOC related information. The result of the CFTC OIG audit will be included in the Council of Inspectors General on Financial Oversight (CIGFO) Working Group audit of FSOC controls over sensitive information. As of March 31, 2012, fieldwork for this audit was complete. In April 2012 the CFTC-OIG will provide CIGFO with its results using a common data collection instrument.

2.   *Preliminary Investigation Regarding Position Limits Rulemaking Efforts*

In August and September 2011 we received anonymous allegations of misconduct in connection with the position limits rulemaking efforts undertaken pursuant to the Dodd-Frank Act. We completed our preliminary investigation in February 2012 and published our report to the OIG website.

The allegations, all anonymous, were that the team leader for the position limits rulemaking "sneakily" got himself appointed team lead and thereafter removed from the team the most experienced members in order to use only newer CFTC employees that he could manipulate (presumably in order to improperly influence the substance of the rule). The team leader was also alleged to have engaged in improper communications with external entities while working on the rule. The anonymous allegations additionally asserted that the position limits rulemaking would be unworkable because it was not compatible with the large swaps trader reporting rule. Finally, the source or sources of the anonymous allegations expressed a fear of retaliation.

The allegations encompassed potentially criminal activity in a recent mission-critical undertaking required under the Dodd-Frank Act because they generally alleged dishonest conduct and corruption. We determined to take a closer look in order to determine whether to make any referrals for formal criminal investigation.

We conducted 21 interviews with members of the large swaps trader and position limits rulemaking teams, with staff consulted by the team lead during the rulemaking process, and with Agency management and the Chairman.

We found no evidence to sustain a preliminary finding of wrongdoing by any individual connected with the position limits and large swaps trader reporting rulemakings. Specifically, we found no evidence to indicate that the position limits rulemaking team leader "sneakily" had himself appointed team lead. Witnesses uniformly asserted that the need to create a separate position limits rulemaking team arose from the volume of work involved with the position limits rule. Witnesses also were uniform in their assertion that the person who was appointed team lead for the position limits rulemaking team had superior experience with position limits, and did not ask for the assignment.

We found no evidence that the position limits rulemaking team was managed by the team lead so as to disregard more experienced CFTC employees in favor of less experienced ones that could be manipulated. Witnesses told us that team members – both experienced and less experienced – came and went with varying degrees of participation throughout the process, both due to the fact their involvement was issue-specific, and in order to keep up with ongoing CFTC work. The team members involved with drafting – the most time-consuming task – was comprised of one lawyer and one economist each with over 10 years financial regulatory experience; along with one lawyer with roughly two years industry experience dealing specifically with energy trading and fewer than two years financial regulatory experience; and one economist with fewer than two years' experience. The core drafting team was small of necessity, as it would be time consuming to coordinate drafting and review by a large group and still meet deadlines. In addition, witness interviews as well as our examination of numerous email generated during the position limits rulemaking process show the team lead consulted not only with the other team members, but also with CFTC employees with over 20 years' experience throughout the process.

Finally, witnesses uniformly stressed that the position limits rulemaking, more so than most other rulemakings, was heavily influenced throughout by the Chairman and Commissioners, with more than one witness stating that the team lead's influence on policy for this particular rule was somewhat limited due to the Commission's direct involvement.

We also found no evidence of improper communications with external sources; however, this allegation was vague. The CFTC documented over 100 meetings with external sources during the course of the position limits rulemaking process. No witness was aware of any improper communications.

We found no evidence that the position limits rulemaking is fatally flawed due to its incompatibility with the large swaps trader reporting rulemaking. The two rules are interrelated, but the swaps large trader reporting rule is broader in the information collected. Information collected from large swaps traders will enable the CFTC to see the entire market (in addition to being used to implement and enforce position limits in accord with the Dodd-Frank Act). Throughout the rulemaking process, Commissioners publicly acknowledged the potential complexity of the interrelation between these two rules, and acknowledged that large swaps trader reporting necessarily would be subject to later adjustment to facilitate both the calculation and enforcement of any position limits.

Witnesses told us that data coordination issues came to a head as the position limits rulemaking neared completion. Eventually it was determined that assuring the collection of adequate data to establish and enforce position limits would be worked out during the implementation stage of large swaps trader reporting. Based on our interviews we did not conclude that corruption, incompetence, or misconduct by CFTC staff contributed to these issues.

Finally, we found no evidence that CFTC employees in DMO who have raised issues or complained to management regarding the position limits rulemaking have been subjected to retaliation. CFTC employees working on the large swaps trader and position limits rulemakings seemed to have their preferred team lead throughout the rulemaking process for position limits and large swaps trader reporting, with some praising the team lead for large swaps trader reporting and others favoring the team lead for position limits. Moreover, we encountered witnesses who disliked or had some degree of disagreement with each team leader's management style. However, more than one witness told us that, when issues regarding the team leads were brought to the attention of DMO management, the response was effective and there was no retaliation.

Due to the uniform quality of information received from CFTC employees and management, we did not take steps to refer this matter for further investigation.

3.   A Review of Cost-Benefit Analyses Performed by the Commodity Futures Trading Commission in Connection with Rulemakings Undertaken Pursuant to the Dodd-Frank Act

CFTC OIG reviewed the formulation of cost benefit analyses for four notices of proposed rulemakings recently published by the Commodity Futures Trading Commission. We undertook this review at the request of ten members of the Senate Committee on Banking, Housing, and Urban Affairs. The request issued May 4, 2011, and requested our response by June 13, 2011.

The four rules addressed: 1) the treatment of segregated funds of swaps customers; 2) derivatives clearing organization risk management requirements; 3) swaps relationship documentation requirements; and 4) core principles for swap execution facilities. Three of the proposed rules were published in the Federal Register in January and February of this year. The proposed rule addressing the treatment of segregated funds of swaps customers was issued by the Commission in April 2011.

In order to complete this review, we reviewed drafts of the cost-benefit analyses for the four proposed rules, as well as staff e-mail and internal memoranda. In addition, we conducted interviews with 28 CFTC employees at various staff and management levels who were involved with the cost-benefit analyses processes for the four rules. Multiple interviews were conducted with some employees.

Objectives and Methodology

In this review we sought to examine six factors pertaining to the Agency's cost-benefit analyses:

A.   The quantitative methodologies the agency uses to evaluate the costs and benefits of proposed rules and the effects those rules could have on job creation and economic growth;

B.   The qualitative methods the agency uses to categorize or rank the effects of proposed rules;

C.   The extent to which the agency considers alternative approaches to its proposed rules;

D.   The extent to which the agency examines the costs, benefits, and economic impact of reasonable alternatives to its proposed rules;

E.   The extent to which the agency seeks public input and expertise in evaluating the costs, benefits, and economic impact of its proposed rules, and the extent to which the agency incorporates the public input into its proposed rules; and

F.   The extent to which the economic analysis performed by the agency with respect to its proposed rulemakings is transparent and the results are reproducible.

In order to complete the investigation, we reviewed drafts of the cost-benefit analyses for the four proposed rules, staff email, and internal memoranda. In addition, we conducted interviews with 28 CFTC employees at staff and various management levels who were involved (or were reported to us as involved) with the cost-benefit analyses processes for the four rules.

Summary of Findings and Recommendations

Prior to publication of the four proposed rules, the Office of General Counsel and Office of Chief Economist created a uniform methodology for cost-benefit analysis for use with all proposed rulemakings under Dodd-

Frank. That methodology set out in some detail the types of qualitative considerations that might inform a cost-benefit analysis, encouraged the use of both qualitative and quantitative data, and included a template for everyone to follow.

While the methodology initially adopted by the Office of General Counsel and the Office of Chief Economist would permit a detailed and thorough approach to the task, in the three earlier rules we examined it appears the Commission generally adopted a "one size fits all" approach to section 15(a) compliance without giving significant regard to the deliberations addressing idiosyncratic cost and benefit issues that were shaping each rule, and often addressed in the preamble. In fact, although the development of a uniform methodology appeared to be an equal effort between the Office of General Counsel and the Office of Chief Economist, at the outset of the rulemaking efforts the cost-benefit analyses involved less input from the Office of Chief Economist, with the Office of General Counsel taking a dominant role. For the three proposed rules we reviewed that were published in January or February 2011, the cost-benefit analyses were drafted by Commission staff in divisions other than the Office of Chief Economist. In these earlier rulemakings, staff from the Office of Chief Economist did review the drafts, but their edits were not always accepted. In one rulemaking, the Office of Chief Economist did not participate at all.

For the more recent cost-benefit analysis accompanying the proposed segregation/bankruptcy rule, we were pleased with the cost-benefit discussion. Although staff told us this rule was different with regard to cost considerations from the start, they also told us the cost-benefit analysis section was influenced by concerns voiced this year regarding cost-benefit analyses, including an earlier CFTC OIG report addressing cost-benefit considerations in connection with Dodd-Frank rulemakings.

With regard to the segregation/bankruptcy rule, the only deficiencies we detected, based on our review, were somewhat minor. We noted both the lack of clarification of the role of Paperwork Reduction Act costs in the context of the cost-benefit analysis, and the lack of quantified costs to the Agency to implement the regulation. Because the Agency currently includes with its budget requests amounts necessary to implement the Dodd-Frank Act, we believe these costs could also be discussed in the context of Dodd-Frank rulemakings. We believe internal Agency costs, including opportunity costs, are relevant because they may influence the Commission's decisions when faced with regulatory alternatives.

4.   An Investigation Regarding Cost-Benefit Analyses Performed by the Commodity Futures Trading Commission in Connection with Rulemakings Undertaken Pursuant to the Dodd-Frank Act

Background

In March 2011 OIG received a request from the Chairman of the House Committee on Agriculture and from the Chairman of the House Subcommittee on General Farm Commodities and Risk Management, for an investigation into cost-benefit analyses performed by the CFTC in connection with four proposed rules under the Dodd-Frank Act:

1.   Further Defining "Swap Dealer", "Security-based Swap Dealer," "Major Swap Participant," "Major Security-based Swap Participant," and "Eligible Contract Participant," 75 FR 80174 (December 21, 2010) (Joint proposed rule; proposed interpretations) ;

2. Confirmation, Portfolio Reconciliation, Compression Requirements for Swap Dealers and Major Swap Participants, 75 FR 81519 (December 28, 2010) (Notice of proposed rulemaking);

3. Core Principles and Other Requirements for Designated Contract Markets, 75 FR 80572 (December 22, 2010) (Notice of proposed rulemaking);

4. Regulations Establishing and Governing the Duties of Swap Dealers and Major Swap Participants, 75 FR 71397 (November 23, 2010) (Notice of proposed rulemaking).

Objectives and Methodology

In addition to specifying four rules for examination, the Chairman of the House Committee on Agriculture and the Chairman of the Subcommittee on General Farm Commodities and Risk Management set out eight areas of specific inquiry to be addressed:

1. The methodologies the CFTC uses to evaluate costs and benefits;

2. Whether the sequence by which rules are proposed impacts the CFTC's ability to adequately evaluate costs and benefits;

3. The extent to which, in light of budget constraints, the CFTC has sought outside input and expertise in evaluating costs and benefits;

4. The extent to which the CFTC has evaluated and distinguished the costs and benefits of proposed regulations on market participants of diverse sizes and from diverse sectors. For example, did the CFTC give consideration to the costs and benefits a "Swap Dealer" designation would have for non-bank, non-financial companies in addition to large global financial institutions?

5. The extent to which the CFTC gives special consideration to evaluating the costs and benefits for small businesses;

6. The amount of time, on average, that Commission staff spends per rule evaluating costs and benefits as required by 15(a);

7. When one proposed rule is highly dependent on another, as is often the case in Title VII, the extent to which the CFTC gives consideration to the impact preceding or subsequent rules may have on the costs or the benefits of the rule under consideration;

8. The impact the current statutory deadline of Title VII has on the Commission's ability to conduct meaningful cost-benefit analysis and the extent to which an extension of the statutory deadline would improve the Commission's ability to consider the costs associated with proposed rules

Because specific misconduct was not alleged and specific targets were not named, we treated this as a review, rather than an investigation designed to support recommended adverse action against any individual.

In order to complete our work, we reviewed drafts of the cost-benefit analyses for the four proposed rules, staff email, and internal memoranda. In addition, we conducted interviews with 24 CFTC employees at staff and various management levels who were involved (or were reported to us as involved) with the cost-benefit analyses processes for the four rules. We issued our report on April 15, 2011.

Summary of Findings and Recommendations

We found that although the development of a uniform cost-benefit analysis methodology prepared in connection with the Dodd-Frank rulemakings appeared to be an equal effort between the Office of General Counsel and the Office of Chief Economist, in practice the cost-benefit analyses involved less input from the Office of Chief Economist, with the Office of General Counsel taking a dominant role. For the four rules we reviewed, the cost-benefit analyses were drafted by Commission staff in divisions other than the Office of Chief Economist. Staff from the Office of Chief Economist did review the drafts, but their edits were not always accepted. To a greater or lesser extent for the four examined rules, the Office of General Counsel appeared to have the greater "say" in the proposed cost-benefit analyses, and appeared to rely heavily on an historic (and somewhat stripped down) analytical approach. It appeared clear to us that a more robust process was clearly permitted under the cost-benefit guidance issued by the Office of General Counsel and the Office of Chief Economist, and we believed a more robust approach would be desirable, with greater input from the Office of Chief Economist.

Following issuance of our report, the Agency created updated guidance for cost-benefit analyses for use with final rulemakings under Dodd-Frank. We note the updated guidance with approval and continue to recommend that the Office of Chief Economist take on an enhanced or greater role under both the existing methodology and any future methodologies for cost-benefit analyses for both proposed and final rules under the Commodity Exchange Act.

Office of Inspector General
Department of Housing and Urban Development

The U.S. Department of Housing and Urban Development (HUD) Inspector General is one of the original 12 Inspectors General authorized under the Inspector General Act of 1978. The HUD Office of Inspector General (HUD OIG) strives to make a difference in HUD's performance and accountability. HUD OIG has a strong commitment to its statutory mission of detecting and preventing fraud, waste, and abuse and promoting the effectiveness and efficiency of government operations.

While organizationally located within HUD, HUD OIG operates independently with separate budget authority. Its independence allows for clear and objective reporting to HUD's Secretary and to Congress. HUD's primary mission is to improve housing and expand opportunities for families seeking to improve their quality of life. HUD does this through a variety of housing and community development programs aimed at helping Americans nationwide obtain affordable housing. These programs are funded through a $45 billion annual budget and Federal Housing Administration (FHA) mortgage insurance for single-family and multifamily properties, which is self-funded through mortgage insurance premiums.

The past several years have seen enormous and damaging developments in the mortgage market:

- The dissolution of the subprime and Alt-A loan markets;

- Dramatic drops in housing prices in most areas of the country;

- A related rise in defaults and foreclosures;

- Financial insecurity in the mortgage-backed securities markets represented by the government takeover of Fannie Mae and Freddie Mac;

- The collapse of credit markets; and

- As a primary vehicle to address these issues, an urgent reliance on FHA to bolster the mortgage market.

While there are other programs at HUD that are being used in a significant way to help stimulate the economy (for example, billions of dollars in new funding to Community Development Block Grants, increased public housing assistance, etc.), which are also vulnerable to fraudulent and abusive activities, our focus has remained on the FHA program due to the mortgage crisis and an increased reliance on HUD to resolve foreclosure matters at this critical juncture.

The current degree of FHA predominance in the market is unparalleled. To put the FHA issues into perspective, we recently stated in testimony to Congress that, through the magnitude of our work in auditing and investigating many facets of the FHA programs over the course of many years, OIG has had and continues to have concerns regarding the ability of FHA's systems and infrastructure to adequately perform its current requirements and services. These concerns were expressed by OIG to FHA through audits and reports regarding a wide spectrum of areas before the program's current influx of loans and before considering the many proposals that expanded its reach. OIG continues to remain concerned regarding FHA's ability and capacity to oversee the newly generated business. Some of these are long-standing concerns that go back to unresolved issues highlighted in our work products from as far back as the early to mid-1990s.

The FHA Mutual Mortgage Insurance (MMI) fund has not met the statutory 2 percent requirements for the last 3 years. In addition, for the first time ever, HUD's fiscal year 2013 budget included an appropriations request of $688 million to cover a possible shortfall of the MMI fund.

OIG is concerned that increases in demand to the FHA program are having collateral implications for the integrity of the Government National Mortgage Association (Ginnie Mae) mortgage-backed securities (MBS) program, including the potential for increases in fraud in that program. Ginnie Mae securities are the only MBS to carry the full faith and credit guaranty of the United States. If an issuer fails to make the required pass-through payment of principal and interest to MBS investors, Ginnie Mae is required to assume responsibility for it. Typically, Ginnie Mae defaults the issuers and assumes control of the issuers' MBS pools. Like FHA, Ginnie Mae has seen an increase in its market share. From a different vantage point, the industry has noted that Ginnie Mae's struggle to keep pace with FHA could also reduce liquidity in the housing market at a critical moment.

A significant problem facing FHA and the lenders it works with is the fallout from decreasing home values. This condition increases the risk of default, abandonment, and foreclosure and makes it difficult for FHA to resell the properties. A major cause for concern is that even as FHA endorsement levels meet or exceed previous peaks in its program history, FHA defaults have already exceeded those of previous years. This issue reinforces the importance for FHA-approved lenders to maintain solid underwriting standards and quality control processes to withstand severe adverse economic conditions.

Until recently, FHA's market share remained quite low as lenders heavily marketed conventional subprime loans. The tightening credit market has increased FHA's position as a loan insurer and, with that comes an increase in lenders and brokers seeking to do business with the Federal program and an overall concern regarding some of these loan originators.

Many "traditional" fraud schemes continue to affect FHA and are described below:

Loan Origination Fraud

This fraud includes fraudulent and substantially inaccurate income, assets and employment information; false loan applications, false credit letters and reports; false gift letters; seller-funded down payments; concealed cash transactions; straw buyers; flipping; kickbacks; cash-out schemes; fraud rings; and inadequate or fraudulent underwriting activities. While these types of mortgage fraud schemes continue to operate, changing market conditions have generated new or variant schemes.

Rescue or Foreclosure Fraud

Recent trends show that certain individuals in the industry are preying on desperate and vulnerable homeowners who are facing foreclosure. Some improper activities include equity skimming (whereby the homeowner is approached and offered an opportunity to get out of financial trouble by the promise to pay off the mortgage or to receive a sum of money when the property is sold; the property is then deeded to the unscrupulous individual, who may charge the homeowner rent and then fails to make the mortgage payment, thereby causing the property to go into foreclosure) and lease or buy-back plans (wherein the homeowner is deceived into signing over title with the belief that he or she may remain in the house as a renter and eventually buy back the property; however, the terms are so unrealistic that buy-back is impossible, and the homeowner loses possession, with the new title holder walking away with most or all of the equity).

Appraisal Fraud

This fraud is typically central to every loan origination fraud and includes deliberately fraudulent appraisals (substantially misrepresented properties, fictitious properties, bogus comparables), inflated appraisals (designed to "hit the numbers"), or both; appraiser kickbacks; and appraiser coercion.

Identity Theft

Identity theft often includes the use of bogus, invalid, or misused Social Security numbers and may include the involvement of illegal aliens, false ownership documents, or certifications.

Bankruptcy Fraud

Typically, Chapter 7 bankruptcy petitions are filed in lieu of Chapter 13 petitions on behalf of debtors; however, property sales information is fraudulently withheld from the bankruptcy court, and the properties are leased back to the debtors at inflated rents. The debtors' property ownership and equity are stripped from them.

Home Equity Conversion Mortgage (Reverse Mortgage) Fraud

FHA reverse mortgages are a new and potentially vulnerable area for fraud perpetrators. We are aware that the larger loan limits can be attractive to exploiters of the elderly, whether it is by third parties or family members, who seek to strip equity from senior homeowners.

The tasks before HUD OIG continue to be daunting: addressing the elements of fraud that were involved in the collapse of the mortgage market; monitoring the rollout of new FHA loan products to reduce exploitation of program vulnerabilities; and combating perpetrators of fraud, including those who have migrated from the subprime markets, who would exploit FHA loan programs. The consequences of the current mortgage crisis, its worldwide economic implications, and the resulting pressures placed on HUD and OIG could not have come at a more inopportune time. HUD, as a whole, has had significant new leadership responsibilities over the last 7 years in rebuilding communities devastated by disasters (for example, lower Manhattan post-September 11th; the Gulf Coast region after hurricanes Katrina, Rita and Wilma; the Galveston area after recent hurricanes; California fires; and Midwest flooding) that have added tens of billions of dollars in new program funds that require quick distribution and keen oversight.

Recent HUD OIG Work

As part of HUD OIG's nationwide effort to review the foreclosure practices of FHA-approved servicers and lenders, we reviewed foreclosure and claim processes of the five largest FHA mortgage servicers (Bank of America, Wells Fargo Bank, CitiMortgage, JP Morgan Chase, and Ally Financial, Incorporated). HUD OIG internally issued draft memorandums for each of the lenders reviewed. OIG performed these reviews due to reported allegations made in the fall of 2010 that national mortgage servicers were engaged in widespread questionable foreclosure practices involving the use of foreclosure "mills" and a practice known as "robosigning" of sworn documents in thousands of foreclosures throughout the United States. As part of this process, HUD OIG enlisted the assistance of the U.S. Department of Justice's (DOJ) Civil Division to facilitate any possible litigation under the False Claims Act or other statute. DOJ issued Civil Investigative Demands upon two servicers to obtain testimony from servicer employees after they refused to make employees available. We shared our internal drafts with DOJ, which used our reviews and analysis in negotiating a settlement agreement with the five servers reviewed.

On February 9, 2012, DOJ and 49 State attorneys general announced a proposed settlement of $25 billion with the five servicers for their reported violations of foreclosure requirements. As part of the settlement agreement, which has been signed by the five servicers and submitted to Federal District Court for entry of a Consent Decree, as discussed below, each of the five servicers will pay a portion of the settlement to the United States and also must undertake certain consumer relief activities. The settlement agreement described tentative credits that each mortgage servicer will receive for modifying loans, including principal reduction and refinancing, and established a monitoring committee and a monitor to ensure compliance with agreed-upon servicing standards and the consumer relief provisions.

HUD OIG is preparing a summary memorandum detailing each of the five servicers' allocated shares of payment due pursuant to the settlement agreement. This memorandum will also make recommendations to correct weaknesses discussed in the five separate servicer memorandums.

DOJ, HUD, HUD OIG, and 49 State attorneys general announced their landmark $25 billion agreement with the Nation's five largest mortgage servicers to address mortgage loan servicing and foreclosure abuses. The Federal Government and State attorneys general filed in U.S. District Court in the District of Columbia proposed consent judgments with Bank of America Corporation, J.P. Morgan Chase & Co., Wells Fargo & Company, CitiMortgage, and Ally Financial, Incorporated, to resolve violations of State and Federal law.

The unprecedented joint agreement is the largest Federal-State civil settlement ever obtained and is the result of extensive investigations by Federal agencies, including DOJ, HUD, and HUD OIG; State attorneys general; and State banking regulators across the country.

The consent judgments provide the details of the servicers' financial obligations under the agreement, which include (1) payments to borrowers whose homes were foreclosed upon and more than $20 billion in consumer relief, (2) new standards the servicers will be required to implement regarding mortgage loan servicing and foreclosure practices, and (3) the oversight and enforcement authorities of the independent settlement monitor. In addition, the consent judgments require the servicers to collectively dedicate $20 billion toward various forms of financial relief to homeowners, including (1) reducing the principal on loans for borrowers who are delinquent or at imminent risk of default and owe more on their mortgages than their homes are worth, (2) refinancing loans for borrowers who are current on their mortgages but who owe more on their mortgage than their homes are worth, (3) forbearance of principal for unemployed borrowers, (4) anti-blight provisions, (5) short sales, (6) transitional assistance, and (7) benefits for service members. The consent judgments' consumer relief requirements include varying amounts of partial credit the servicers will receive for every dollar spent on the required relief activities. Because servicers will receive only partial credit for many of the relief activities, the agreement will result in benefits to borrowers in excess of $20 billion.

The servicers are required to complete 75 percent of their consumer relief obligations within 2 years and 100 percent within 3 years.

In addition to the $20 billion in financial relief for borrowers, the consent judgments require the servicers to pay $5 billion in cash to the Federal and State governments. Approximately $1.5 billion of this payment will be used to establish a Borrower Payment Fund to provide cash payments to borrowers whose homes were sold or taken in foreclosure between January 1, 2008, and December 31, 2011, and who meet other criteria. In addition, the FHA reserve fund will receive approximately $321 million as part of the general servicing agreement, approximately $470 million as part of a separate agreement with Bank of America, and approximately $115 million as part of a separate agreement with CitiMortgage , for a total of approximately $906 million. There is also a provision in the Bank of America agreement whereby FHA could receive up to an additional $850 million should Bank of America fail to meet certain goals related to loan workouts, refinancing, and other measures within 3 years.

A copy of the full reports is available on our website: *www.hudoig.gov.*

	Bank of America	**Wells Fargo**	**CitiMortgage**	**JP Morgan Chase**	**Ally Financial, Incorporated**
Memorandum number	2012-FW-1802	2012-AT-1801	2012-KC-1801	2012-CH-1801	2012-PH-1801
Review scope	10/1/08- 9/30/10 Charlotte, NC	10/1/08- 9/30/10 Fort Mill, SC	10/1/08- 9/30/10 O'Fallon, MO	10/1/08- 9/30/10 Columbus, OH	10/1/08-9/30/10 Fort Washington, PA
Conveyance claims submitted (in the 23 judicial foreclosure States & jurisdictions)	8,973 claims totaling nearly $1.1 billion	14,420 claims totaling about $1.7 billion	5,182 claims totaling nearly $597 million	4,437 claims totaling more than $547 million	1,345 claims totaling $160.5 million

Office of Inspector General
Department of the Treasury

The Department of the Treasury's Office of Inspector General (OIG) was established pursuant to the 1988 amendments to the Inspector General Act of 1978. The Treasury Inspector General is appointed by the President, with the advice and consent of the Senate. Treasury OIG performs independent, objective reviews of Treasury programs and operations, except for those of the Internal Revenue Service (IRS) and the Troubled Asset Relief Program (TARP), and keeps the Secretary of the Treasury and Congress fully informed.[1] Treasury OIG is comprised of five divisions: (1) Office of Audit, (2) Office of Investigations, (3) Office of Small Business Lending Fund Program Oversight, (4) Office of Counsel, and (5) Office of Management. Treasury OIG is headquartered in Washington, DC, and has an audit office in Boston, MA.

The Treasury OIG has oversight responsibility for one federal banking agency--the Office of the Comptroller of the Currency (OCC). OCC is responsible for 1,399 national banks and 637 federal savings associations with total assets of $9.6 trillion, comprising 76 percent of the U.S. banking system. The Treasury OIG also oversees several new offices and functions created by the Dodd-Frank Act such as the Office of Financial Research (OFR), the Federal Insurance Office, and the Offices of Minority and Women Inclusion within Treasury Departmental Offices and OCC. Furthermore, the Treasury OIG oversees certain Treasury functions related to Fannie Mae and Freddie Mac under the Housing and Economic Recovery Act of 2008, to include Treasury's Preferred Stock Purchase Agreement Program for the purpose of maintaining a positive net worth for both entities ($187 billion as of March 31, 2012, covering net worth deficiencies through December 31, 2011). Finally, related to Treasury's role in the economic recovery, the Treasury OIG oversees approximately $24 billion in non-IRS Recovery Act funds.

By statute, the Treasury Inspector General also serves as the Chair of the Council of Inspectors General on Financial Oversight, and as a member of the Recovery Act Accountability and Transparency Board.

Failed Bank Reviews

In 1991, Congress enacted the Federal Deposit Insurance Corporation Improvement Act (FDICIA) amending the Federal Deposit Insurance Act (FDIA). The law was enacted following the failures of about a thousand banks and thrifts from 1986 to 1990, which resulted in billions of dollars in losses to the Deposit Insurance Fund. The amendments require that banking regulators take specified supervisory actions when they identify unsafe or unsound practices or conditions. Also added was a requirement that the Inspector General for the primary federal regulator of a failed financial institution conduct a material loss review (MLR) when the estimated loss to the Deposit Insurance Fund is "material." As part of the MLR, OIG auditors determine the causes of the failure and assess the supervision of the institution, including the implementation of the prompt

---

1   The Treasury Inspector General for Tax Administration performs oversight of IRS, and a Special Inspector General performs oversight of TARP.

corrective action (PCA) provisions of the act.[2] As appropriate, the Treasury OIG also makes recommendations for preventing any such loss in the future.

FDICIA defined a material loss as a loss to the Deposit Insurance Fund that exceeded the greater of $25 million or 2 percent of the institution's total assets. Dodd-Frank redefined the loss threshold amount to the Deposit Insurance Fund triggering a material loss review to a loss that exceeds $200 million for 2010 and 2011, $150 million for 2012 and 2013, and $50 million for 2014 and thereafter (with a provision to temporarily raise the threshold to $75 million in certain circumstances). The act also requires a review of all bank failures with losses under these threshold amounts for the purposes of (1) ascertaining the grounds identified by OCC for appointing FDIC as receiver and (2) determining whether any unusual circumstances exist that might warrant a more in-depth review of the loss. This provision applies to bank failures from October 1, 2009, forward.

From the beginning of the current economic crisis in 2007 through June 30, 2012, FDIC and other banking regulators closed 440 banks and thrifts. One hundred twenty-four (124) of these were Treasury-regulated financial institutions. Of these 124 failures, 54 resulted in a material loss to the Deposit Insurance Fund, so an MLR was required. As of June May 31, 2012, we completed 54 required material loss reviews—28 failed institutions regulated by OCC and 26 failed institutions regulated by the former Office of Thrift Supervision (OTS).[3] In total, the estimated loss to the Deposit Insurance Fund for these 54 failures was $32.9 billion.

Some of our overarching observations from these and other reviews performed by Treasury OIG are summarized below. With respect to the causes of the institutions' failures, we found poor underwriting and overly aggressive growth strategies fueled by volatile and costly wholesale funding (e.g , brokered deposits, Federal Home Loan Bank loans); risky lending products such as option adjustable rate mortgages; high asset concentrations to include commercial real estate loans; and inadequate risk management systems. In addition, the management and boards of these institutions were often not effective in recognizing, monitoring, or managing their risks. The economic recession and the decline in the real estate market were also contributing factors in most of the failures.

With respect to OCC's and the former OTS's supervision, we found that the regulators conducted regular and timely examinations and identified operational problems, but were slow to take timely and aggressive enforcement action. We also found that in rating these institutions, examiners gave too much weight to the fact that the institutions were profitable and their loans were performing and not enough weight given to the amount of risk that these institutions had taken on. We also noted that regulators took the appropriate prompt corrective action actions when warranted but those actions did not save the institutions. We found several banks received TARP funds prior to failure. Treasury's TARP investment in these banks is expected to be lost.

---

2   PCA is a framework of supervisory actions for insured institutions that are not adequately capitalized. It was intended to ensure that action is taken when an institution becomes financially troubled in order to prevent a failure or minimize the resulting losses. These actions become increasingly severe as the institution falls into lower capital categories. The capital categories are well-capitalized, adequately capitalized, undercapitalized, significantly undercapitalized, and critically undercapitalized.

3   Pursuant to the Dodd-Frank Act, the functions of OTS were transferred to OCC, the Federal Deposit Insurance Corporation (FDIC), and Board of Governors of the Federal Reserve System (FRB) on July 21, 2011, and OTS was abolished 90 days later. All OTS functions relating to federal savings associations, all OTS rulemaking authority for federal and state savings associations, and the majority of OTS employees transferred to OCC.

We are currently preparing a summary of common themes related to the causes of failure and supervision of institutions and assessing OCC's actions to strengthen the supervisory process in response to our audit recommendations and on its own initiative.

Review of Treasury's Efforts to Stand Up the Office of Financial Research

As mentioned above, OFR was established within Treasury by the Dodd-Frank Act to support FSOC and its member agencies. We completed a review in June 2012 of Treasury's process to stand up OFR. We reported that, in the 21 months since OFR was created, efforts to establish the office are still in progress. The officials responsible for establishing OFR initially engaged in high-level strategic and organizational planning and sought to hire key personnel. They also focused their attention on developing and facilitating the global acceptance of a Legal Entity Identifier (a universal standard for identifying all parties to financial contracts) while leveraging Treasury to support the office's administrative functions. In Summer 2011, after key operational personnel were brought on board, progress toward establishing a comprehensive implementation planning and project management process accelerated and by April 2012, OFR had a comprehensive implementation plan in place. Concurrent with the development of its comprehensive implementation plan, we noted that OFR also began to develop its analytic and data support for FSOC, and its Research and Analysis Center has sponsored seminars and published two working papers on risk assessment topics. OFR agreed with our recommendation to monitor its progress in carrying out the activities in the comprehensive implementation plan and take actions timely to address any slippages or otherwise make adjustments so as to achieve the objectives and timeframes in the plan.

Review of FSOC's Response to a Congressional Inquiry Related to Raising the Debt Limit (In Progress)

As a part of our oversight responsibilities and to respond to a request by the Ranking Member of the U.S. Senate Committee on Finance received in October 2011 and January 2012, we are conducting a review of FSOC's response to the Ranking Member's inquiries of July and August 2011 regarding the debt limit. Consistent with this request, our objectives are to assess and report on matters related to (1) Treasury's cash projections during July and August 2011, (2) contingency plans developed by FSOC voting member agencies if the debt limit had not been raised or if there was a credit rating downgrade on the United States, (3) FSOC's compliance with statutory requirements for identifying risks and responding to emerging threats to financial stability, and (4) FSOC's reporting on systemic risks surrounding the debt limit.

Congressional Request on Small Community Bank Supervision (In Progress)

The Treasury OIG is reviewing OCC's examination process for small community banks. This work was undertaken at the request of the Chairman of the Senate Committee on Banking, Housing, and Urban Affairs. The work is being coordinated with the OIGs of the other federal banking agencies.

Treasury Management and Performance Challenges Related to Financial Regulation and Economic Analysis

In accordance with the Reports Consolidation Act of 2000, the Treasury Inspector General annually provides the Secretary of the Treasury with his perspective on the most serious management and performance challenges facing the Department. In an October 2011 memorandum to Secretary Geithner, Inspector General Thorson reported two management and performance challenges that were specifically directed towards financial regulation and economic recovery. Those challenges were: Transformation of Financial Regulation and Management of Treasury's Authorities Intended to Support and Improve the Economy.

Transformation of Financial Regulation

With the intention to prevent, or at least minimize, the impact of a future financial sector crisis on the US economy, the Dodd-Frank Act placed a great deal of responsibility within Treasury and on the Secretary of the Treasury. Accordingly, this challenge, among other things, primarily focused on a number of the Dodd-Frank Act mandates related to Treasury. It broadly addressed the challenge of implementing an effective FSOC that timely identifies and strongly responds to emerging risks. It included Treasury's role in successfully standing up the Consumer Financial Protection Bureau. It addressed two new mandated offices to be established within Treasury: the Office of Financial Research and the Federal Insurance Office. It discussed the act's effort to streamline the supervision of depository institutions and holding companies by requiring the transfer the powers and duties of OTS to OCC, FRB, and FDIC. It also discussed the results of two reviews we and the OIGs of FDIC and FRB completed on the planning and the status of the transfer.

This management and performance challenge also included the other regulatory challenges that the Treasury Inspector General had previously reported. Specifically, it acknowledged the number of Treasury-regulated financial institutions that failed since the beginning of the current economic crisis and their multi-billion losses to the Deposit Insurance Fund. With respect to those failures and associated losses, the challenge stated that although many factors contributed to the turmoil in the financial markets, our work found that OCC and the former OTS did not identify early or force timely correction of unsafe and unsound practices by numerous failed institutions under their supervision. Among other things, we also spoke to the irresponsible lending practices of many institutions, including reliance on risky products, such as option adjustable rate mortgages, and degradation of underwriting standards as well as high asset concentrations in commercial real estate and overreliance on unpredictable wholesale funding.

Management of Treasury's Authorities Intended to Support and Improve the Economy

This challenge, among other things, focused on a number of broad authorities the Congress provided to Treasury to address the financial crisis under the Housing and Economic Recovery Act and the Emergency Economic Stabilization Act, both enacted in 2008, the American Recovery and Reinvestment Act of 2009 (Recovery Act), and the Small Business Jobs Act of 2010. It acknowledged that certain authorities in the Housing and Economic Recovery Act and the Emergency Economic Stabilization Act expired, but pointed out the fact that challenges remain in managing Treasury's outstanding investments. To a large extent, Treasury's program administration under these acts have matured, however, investment decisions involving the Small Business Jobs Act programs have only recently been completed. Small Business Jobs Act programs include Small Business Lending Fund and the State Small Business Credit Initiative.

As a final note, another challenge that the Treasury Inspector General reported for a number of years is Treasury's anti-money laundering and terrorist financing/Bank Secrecy Act enforcement efforts. Among other things, this challenge pointed out our particular concern with respect to ensuring continued cooperation and coordination of all organizations involved in anti-money laundering and combating terrorist financing efforts. Specifically, we expressed our concern that neither the Financial Crimes Enforcement Network nor the Office of Foreign Assets Control has the resources or capability to maintain compliance with their programs without significant help from other organizations, including the financial regulators.

Office of Inspector General
The Federal Deposit Insurance Corporation

The FDIC was created by the Congress in 1933 as an independent agency to maintain stability and public confidence in the nation's banking system by insuring deposits and independently regulating state-chartered, non-member banks. Federal deposit insurance protects depositors from losses due to failures of insured commercial banks and thrifts. According to most recent data, the FDIC insured approximately $7.0 trillion in deposits at 7,357 banks and savings associations, and promoted the safety and soundness of these institutions by identifying, monitoring, and addressing risks to which they are exposed. The FDIC was the primary federal regulator for 4,597 of the insured institutions. An equally important role for the FDIC, especially in light of the recent financial crisis, is as receiver for failed institutions. The FDIC is responsible for resolving the institutions and managing and disposing of remaining assets.

The FDIC OIG is an independent and objective unit established under the Inspector General Act of 1978, as amended. The FDIC OIG mission is to promote the economy, efficiency, and effectiveness of FDIC programs and operations, and protect against fraud, waste, and abuse. In doing so, we can assist and augment the FDIC's contribution to stability and public confidence in the nation's financial system. We have continued to undertake a comprehensive body of work during the past year to carry out that mission.

Focus of FDIC OIG Work Shifts from Institution Failures to Resolution and Receivership Activities

The FDIC OIG's audit work since issuance of the first Council of Inspectors General on financial Oversight (CIGFO) annual report has included our mandatory reviews of failed FDIC-insured institutions, although the volume of such work has lessened considerably, given fewer failures and changes in the threshold for conducting such reviews, as outlined in the Dodd-Frank Wall Street Reform and Consumer Protection Act (Dodd-Frank Act). As discussed in the previous CIGFO Annual Report, this body of work, along with corresponding supervisory enhancements that the FDIC has made continues to have a positive impact on the FDIC's supervision of financial institutions.

When an institution fails, the FDIC faces challenges as the receiver for the institution's assets and liabilities. Since January 1, 2008, the FDIC has been appointed as receiver for 437 failed institutions, with total assets at inception in excess of $670 billion. To fund the cost of resolutions and pay insured depositors when a bank fails, the FDIC maintains the Deposit Insurance fund (DIF), which has experienced an estimated loss of more than $88 billion as a result of these 437 failures.

In resolving failed institutions, the FDIC markets failing institutions to all interested and qualified bidders, offering multiple alternative resolution structures. The FDIC's preferred approach is to sell all or a part of the failing institution's assets to an open financial institution that also assumes the failed institution's deposit liabilities. To incentivize the acquiring institution to take on some of the assets of the failed institution, the FDIC may enter into a risk-sharing arrangement known as a shared-loss agreement (SLA). Any remaining unsold assets become part of the receivership. The FDIC may later market and sell those residual assets to qualified purchasers through a variety of means, including a structured asset sale transaction, a second type of risk-sharing arrangement.

Over the past year, the FDIC OIG has been able to shift some audit attention from examining institution failures to the Corporation's resolution and receivership management activities, including the SLAs and structured asset sale transactions, as discussed below. Of note, on May 16, 2012, FDIC Inspector General Jon Rymer testified at a hearing on *Oversight of the FDIC's Structured Transaction Program* before the Committee on Financial Services, Subcommittee on Oversight and Investigations, U.S. House of Representatives, to share his views on these activities.

Shared Loss Agreements: An SLA, which is part of a purchase and assumption agreement with an acquiring institution, includes provisions under which the FDIC agrees to absorb a portion of the losses experienced by an acquiring institution on a specified pool of assets. While the FDIC generally absorbs 80 percent of certain losses, in some SLAs during the crisis, the FDIC agreed to absorb up to 95 percent of certain losses. As of March 31, 2012, the FDIC reported that it had entered into 285 SLAs with an original principal balance of $212.7 billion in assets.

Given the number of SLAs and the associated risks to the DIF, we initially identified individual, large SLA transactions that, in our judgment, presented significant financial risk to the FDIC, and from which we believed we could derive lessons that would help management to develop and improve controls. We conducted seven audits of individual SLAs, resulting in reports containing 93 recommendations, of which numerous recommendations related to the establishment of program level controls. Questioned costs in these audits totaled about $84.5 million and funds put to better use totaled nearly $410,000. Management has taken responsive action to the findings and recommendations in these reports.

With the eventual development by FDIC management of more robust internal control structures at the transaction level, we later examined the FDIC's controls at a higher program level. We issued a report on the FDIC's monitoring of SLAs, in which we discussed the evolution of the program since its inception and the steps the FDIC was taking to ensure acquiring institutions' compliance with the agreements.

We determined that the FDIC had devoted high-level management attention to the quickly expanding SLA program. The Corporation had also substantially increased staff, engaged contractors, and developed procedures and systems to manage the associated workload and risks. As a result of these efforts, the FDIC had established a number of controls and processes to monitor and ensure that acquiring institutions complied with the terms and conditions of the SLAs. The FDIC was also taking steps to enhance information security of its SLA data resources; guidance to acquiring institutions regarding commercial loan modifications; tracking of questioned claims and processes for ensuring corrective action; and oversight of acquiring institutions to more promptly prevent or detect instances of non-compliance.

However, as our report noted, in any program of this size, there would be emerging issues and risks that require monitoring and attention. In that regard, we made five recommendations to the FDIC related to the timeliness of contractor task orders, the efficiency of evaluating contractor performance, the consistency of acquiring institution monitoring efforts, and the sufficiency of guidance for pursuing and reporting recoveries and monitoring non-compliant acquiring institutions. These recommendations were intended to strengthen the SLA program, and FDIC management agreed to take responsive action.

Structured Asset Sale Transactions: Not all assets from the failed institutions are sold to acquiring institutions. These residual assets consist largely of distressed and non-performing single-family and commercial real estate loans and real property that pass into and are held in FDIC receiverships. The FDIC's objective is to return these assets to the private sector as promptly as possible, while maximizing the net present value return from the sale and minimizing loss to the DIF, consistent with the FDIC's statutory obligations.

The FDIC uses multiple vehicles to sell these assets, among which are structured asset sale transactions. Structured asset sale transactions involve pools of assets from one or more FDIC receiverships. The FDIC sells or contributes assets to a limited liability company (LLC) formed by the FDIC as receiver. These transactions are competitively bid to prequalified purchasers. The receiver then sells an interest in the LLC to a private third-party, which manages the LLC. The receiver retains either an equity interest in the LLC or a participation interest in the net cash collected through the servicing and liquidation of the LLC's assets. Once ownership of the assets is conveyed to the LLC, control over the LLC is passed to the private third-party. The FDIC, acting as receiver for failed banks, reported that it has consummated 32 structured sale transactions involving 42,314 assets with a total unpaid principal balance of approximately $25.5 billion, as of April 25, 2012.

To date, the FDIC OIG has completed audits of two structured asset sale transactions. We contracted with Clifton Larson Allen LLP to conduct these audits and assess the acquiring institution's compliance with the agreements and the FDIC's monitoring of the agreements. The first audit involved 1,112 individual assets with an unpaid principal balance at closing of $1.167 billion. The second audit involved 101 individual assets with an unpaid principal balance at closing of $4.4 billion, and an advance funding mechanism of up to $1.15 billion to fund the construction of incomplete buildings and provide other asset-related working capital.

With respect to compliance with the agreements, both reports included questioned costs relating to servicing expenses and management fees. In the case of one of the LLCs, questioned costs of $634,412 consisted primarily of expenses incurred by the LLC that were inappropriately treated as liquidation costs instead of servicing costs covered by the management fee. Questioned costs also included management fees charged on assets that had no value but that had not been written-off by the Managing Member. The report also noted that the FDIC could prospectively achieve an estimated $3.1 million in funds put to better use by addressing issues involving the LLC's accounting practices for servicing costs paid to contractors and for worthless assets. The second audit resulted in $6.3 million in questioned costs, consisting primarily of unallowable servicing costs, such as professional services provided by real estate development firms, and travel, meals, and entertainment expenses that were prohibited under the terms of the structured asset sale agreement. The FDIC committed to take action on the recommendations that we made in these two reports.

We had also determined that the FDIC's controls for monitoring structured asset sales needed improvement. During or subsequent to our field work on the second audit, the FDIC advised us that it had either established or planned a number of control improvements related to its structured asset sale transactions, including, issuing policies and procedures for monitoring structured asset sale transactions, engaging compliance monitoring contractors to perform periodic compliance reviews of LLCs and Managing Members, assigning additional resources for monitoring, and beginning a process for quarterly reporting to the FDIC's Audit Committee, an FDIC Board–level committee.

We intend to continue audits of individual SLA and structured asset sale transactions going forward because of the dollar value of the transactions and to provide a deterrent effect as it relates to the risk of fraud. However, we also anticipate a shift in the focus of our work regarding structured asset sale transactions. That is, as the structured asset sale program matures and as resources permit, we plan to elevate our focus to a program-level review that assesses overall monitoring and oversight controls.

FDIC OIG Investigations Target Financial Institution Fraud

Investigative work at both open and closed banks complements the audits and evaluations we have conducted and provides additional insights into the causes for institution failures and the control weaknesses that allow perpetrators of fraud to pursue illegal acts undermining the integrity of the financial services industry. Our office is committed to partnerships with other OIGs, the Department of Justice, the Federal Bureau of Investigation, and other state and local law enforcement agencies in pursuing such criminal acts and helping to deter fraud, waste, and abuse. The OIG also actively participates on numerous mortgage fraud and other financial fraud working groups nationwide to keep current with new threats and fraudulent schemes that can undermine the integrity of the FDIC's operations and the financial services industry as a whole. These include the Bank Fraud Working Group, Mortgage Fraud Working Group, and Financial Fraud Enforcement Task Force, all spearheaded by the Department of Justice.

Our current caseload includes 225 active investigations. Of these, 110 relate to open bank matters and 115 to closed bank matters. These cases involve fraud and other misconduct on the part of senior bank officials, and include mortgage and commercial loan fraud exposed by turmoil in the housing, commercial real estate, and lending industries. The perpetrators of such crimes can be those very individuals entrusted with governance responsibilities at the institutions—directors and bank officers. In other cases, individuals providing professional services to the banks and customers, others working inside the bank, and customers themselves are principals in fraudulent schemes. Other investigations include cases involving misrepresentations of FDIC insurance or affiliation, concealment of assets, and computer crimes. The OIG's success in all such investigations contributes to ensuring the continued safety and soundness of the nation's banks and the strength of the financial system as a whole.

FDIC OIG investigative results over the past two semiannual reporting periods include the following: 157 indictments; 89 arrests; 122 convictions, and potential monetary recoveries (fines, restitution, and asset forfeitures) of more than $4.0 billion, of which $3.5 billion reflects ordered restitution from one case relating to the failure of Colonial Bank, Montgomery, AL.

Collaborative Efforts with OIG Colleagues Address Issues of Mutual Interest

As a member of CIGFO, the FDIC OIG has responsibilities under the Dodd-Frank Act to monitor the FDIC's involvement on the Financial Stability Oversight Council and to join with other CIGFO members to address cross-cutting issues impacting the financial system. The FDIC OIG was the lead agency in one such joint effort to examine the controls and protocols that FSOC and its member agencies have put in place to ensure that FSOC-collected information, deliberations, and decisions are safeguarded from unauthorized disclosure.

During the past year, we also partnered with the Department of the Treasury and Federal Reserve OIGs on two different types of reviews. The first focused on prompt regulatory action-related sections of the Federal Deposit Insurance Act. The second addressed certain aspects of the transfer of Office of Thrift Supervision functions to the FDIC, Office of the Comptroller of the Currency (OCC), and Board of Governors of the Federal Reserve system (FRB), as required under the Dodd-Frank Act. (See pages 6 -7 for a discussion of these joint efforts)

Ongoing FDIC OIG Work Addresses Areas of Congressional Interest

As of the date of issuance of this annual CIGFO report, we were also engaged in responding to two different areas of Congressional interest. The first relates to a Congressional mandate that the FDIC OIG conduct a comprehensive study on the impact of the failure of insured depository institutions and submit a report along with any recommendations to the Congress by January 3, 2013. We are also conducting a second assignment at the request of Senator Tim Johnson, Chairman of the Senate Banking Committee, to review the FDIC's examination process for small community banks. Other financial regulatory OIGs are responding to Senator Johnson as well, and we are coordinating our efforts with them. Both undertakings are described below:

H.R. 2056: On January 3, 2012, President Obama signed H.R. 2056, as amended. This legislation requires that the FDIC IG conduct a comprehensive study on the impact of the failure of insured depository institutions and submit a report to the Congress not later than 1 year after the date of enactment. The report is to contain the results of the study and any recommendations. The legislation further requires that the FDIC Inspector General and the Comptroller General appear before the Committee on Banking, Housing, and Urban Affairs of the Senate and the Committee on Financial Services of the House of Representatives after publication of the study to discuss the results. The scope of the study, as defined in the legislation, must include institutions regulated by the FDIC, the FRB, and the OCC.

The legislation requires that we consult with the Treasury and FRB IGs in conducting the review, and that those IGs will provide documents or other materials we request in order to perform the study. We have coordinated our work closely with them to date and will continue to do so.

We have initiated a series of assignments to address the issues outlined in H.R. 2056. In brief, our work is focusing on the following key areas: Losses and Fair Value Accounting; Appraisals, Allowance for Loan and Lease Loss, and Capital Adequacy; Workouts; Enforcement Orders; Private Capital Investments and FDIC Policy on Capital Investments; and Shared-Loss Agreements.

We will report more extensively on the results of this comprehensive study in next year's annual CIGFO report.

Congressional Request Regarding Small Community Banks: On February 10, 2012, we received a letter from the Chairman of the Senate Banking Committee, Senator Tim Johnson, requesting that our office conduct work related to the FDIC's examination process for small community banks. The Chairman made similar requests to the IGs at the Department of the Treasury, FRB, and National Credit Union Administration.

In response to this request, we have initiated an audit so that we can report on the:

- FDIC's examination process for small community banks, including examination timelines and how the FDIC ensures consistency in the administration of examinations across the country.

- Ability of FDIC-supervised institutions to question examination results, such as through the Office of the Ombudsman, the appeals process, or informal channels, and the frequency and success of such appeals.

We are coordinating our work with fellow financial regulatory OIGs, and will report our results in the next annual CIGFO report.

Please consult *www.fdicig.gov* for more information on the work of the FDIC OIG.

Office of Inspector General
Federal Housing Finance Agency

Background

The Federal Housing Finance Agency's Office of Inspector General ("FHFA-OIG") was established by the Housing and Economic Recovery Act of 2008, and began operations on October 12, 2010. FHFA-OIG conducts, supervises, and coordinates audits, evaluations, investigations, and other activities relating to the programs and operations of the Federal Housing Finance Agency ("FHFA" or the "Agency"), which regulates and supervises the housing-related Government-Sponsored Enterprises ("GSEs"): the Federal National Mortgage Association ("Fannie Mae"), the Federal Home Loan Mortgage Corporation ("Freddie Mac"), and the Federal Home Loan Banks ("FHLBanks"). Since September 2008, FHFA has also served as conservator for Fannie Mae and Freddie Mac (collectively, the "Enterprises").

FHFA-OIG has recorded significant accomplishments over the past year relating to financial oversight. These and other accomplishments are discussed further in FHFA-OIG's Second and Third Semiannual Reports to the Congress, which are available at ***www.fhfaoig.gov***.

FHFA-OIG's Vision and Mission

FHFA-OIG's vision is to be an efficient and effective organization that promotes excellence and trust through its service to FHFA, Congress, the Administration, and the American public.

FHFA-OIG's mission is to:

- Promote the economy, efficiency, and effectiveness of FHFA's programs and operations;

- Prevent and detect fraud, waste, and abuse in those programs and operations; and

- Seek administrative sanctions of, civil recoveries from, and/or criminal prosecutions of those responsible for fraud, waste, and abuse in connection with those programs and operations.

In carrying out its mission, FHFA-OIG:

- Keeps the Director of FHFA, Congress, and the American people fully and currently informed of problems and deficiencies relating to FHFA's programs and operations; and

- Works with FHFA staff and program participants to improve FHFA's programs and operations.

Recent Examples of FHFA-OIG's Financial Oversight Work

FHFA-OIG Office of Evaluations, Report No. EVL-2011-003: Evaluation of FHFA's Role in Negotiating Fannie Mae's and Freddie Mac's Responsibilities in Treasury's Making Home Affordable Program (August 12, 2011)

FHFA-OIG evaluated FHFA's oversight of the Enterprises' participation in the Making Home Affordable Program ("MHA"), a Treasury initiative established in response to the financial crisis. A key part of the MHA is the Home Affordable Modification Program ("HAMP"), which involves servicers agreeing to modify mortgages for borrowers facing imminent default or foreclosure. In early 2009, the Enterprises began participating in HAMP. The Enterprises entered into five-year agreements with Treasury to manage the program and oversee participants' compliance with program requirements. An FHFA-OIG evaluation found that FHFA largely removed itself from overseeing the negotiations of the agreements and did not review the agreements' substance. This lack of engagement may have contributed to the agreements' omission of significant details concerning payments to the Enterprises, the scope of their responsibilities, and processes to resolve differences. As a consequence of the omissions, significant problems developed in these areas almost from the beginning, requiring FHFA and the Enterprises to devote substantial time and resources to resolve ambiguities. FHFA-OIG recommended that FHFA negotiate with Treasury and the Enterprises to develop a dispute resolution process.

FHFA-OIG Office of Evaluations, Report No. EVL-2011-004: Evaluation of FHFA's Oversight of Fannie Mae's Management of Operational Risk (September 23, 2011)

FHFA requires the Enterprises to implement programs to identify, report, and remedy "operational risks," which are risks of loss resulting from failures in people, processes or systems, or from external events (such as foreclosure abuses) and which therefore challenge an Enterprise's safety and soundness. FHFA reported that Fannie Mae had not taken adequate steps to establish an acceptable and effective operational risk management program. FHFA-OIG evaluated FHFA's oversight of Fannie Mae's efforts in this regard.

As Fannie Mae's regulator and conservator, FHFA's authority over the Enterprise is broad and includes the ability to discipline or remove Enterprise personnel to ensure compliance with Agency mandates. Nevertheless, FHFA-OIG found that FHFA has not taken any decisive action to compel Fannie Mae to establish an effective operational risk management program, despite Fannie Mae's continuing failure to do so being known to regulators since at least 2006. FHFA has instead employed ineffective supervisory methods, such as conducting operational risk examinations. Fannie Mae's history of non-compliance leads FHFA-OIG to believe that maximum diligence and forceful action are required to ensure that this occurs. Otherwise, FHFA's safety and soundness examination program, as well as its delegated approach to conservatorship management, may be adversely affected.

FHFA-OIG recommended that FHFA: (1) closely monitor Fannie Mae's implementation of its operational risk management program; (2) take decisive and timely action if Fannie Mae fails to establish an acceptable and effective program by the end of the first quarter of 2012; and (3) ensure Fannie Mae has qualified personnel in place to administer the program appropriately.

FHFA-OIG Office of Evaluations, Report No. EVL-2011-005: Evaluation of Whether FHFA Has Sufficient Capacity to Examine the GSEs (September 23, 2011)

Examinations are FHFA's primary means for supervising and regulating the GSEs. FHFA has critical regulatory responsibilities with respect to the GSEs overall and conservator responsibilities regarding Fannie Mae and Freddie Mac in particular. To satisfy these responsibilities, Congress provided FHFA significant budget and hiring authority. Nonetheless, an FHFA-OIG evaluation found that the Agency has too few examiners to ensure the efficiency and effectiveness of its GSE oversight program; due to examiner shortages, FHFA has scaled back planned work during examinations, and examinations have often taken much longer than expected to complete. Additionally, FHFA-OIG has identified shortfalls in the Agency's examination coverage, particularly in the crucial area of REO. Indeed, a senior FHFA manager acknowledged to FHFA-OIG that examiners too often accept assertions made by Enterprise managers rather than validate such assertions through appropriate transaction testing. This may be related to FHFA having too few examiners to ensure the efficiency and effectiveness of its examination program, making FHFA's early identification of possible risks more challenging.

FHFA-OIG recommended that FHFA: (1) assess the extent to which examination capacity shortfalls may have adversely affected GSE examination quality; (2) assess potential risk mitigation strategies, such as achieving efficiencies in the assignment of examiners or the examination process; (3) monitor the examiner accreditation program's development and implementation, and address any shortfalls; (4) consider using federal agency detailees, retired annuitants, or contractors to augment its examination program in the near- to mid-term; and (4) report periodically to Congress and the public on examiner capacity shortfalls, its progress in overcoming them, and the development and implementation of its examiner accreditation program.

FHFA-OIG Office of Evaluations, Report No. EVL-2011-006: Evaluation of FHFA's Oversight of Freddie Mac's Repurchase Agreement with Bank of America (September 27, 2011)

In December 2010, FHFA approved a $1.35 billion settlement of mortgage repurchase claims that Freddie Mac asserted against Bank of America. In approving the settlement, FHFA relied on Freddie Mac's analysis of the settlement without testing the assumptions underlying the Enterprise's existing loan review process. However, an FHFA-OIG evaluation found that FHFA did not act timely or test concerns raised by an FHFA senior examiner months prior to the settlement about limitations in that loan review process for mortgage repurchase claims. The senior examiner was concerned that the loan review process Freddie Mac used for repurchase claims failed to account adequately for changes in foreclosure patterns among loans originated during the housing boom. According to the senior examiner, this could potentially cost the Enterprise a considerable amount of money. Freddie Mac's internal auditors independently identified concerns about the process and, in June 2011, recommended that the issue be studied further. Following initiation of FHFA-OIG's report, FHFA suspended future Enterprise mortgage repurchase settlements premised on the Freddie Mac loan review process and set in motion activities to test the assumptions underlying the loan review process.

FHFA-OIG recommended that FHFA: (1) act promptly on the specific and significant concerns about Freddie Mac's loan review process referenced above; and (2) ensure that future significant concerns are brought to senior managers' attention, and that they act promptly upon them.

FHFA-OIG Office of Audits, Report No. AUD-2011-004: FHFA's Oversight of Default-Related Legal Services (September 30, 2011)

In 1997, Fannie Mae created a Retained Attorney Network ("RAN") to acquire default-related legal services associated with foreclosure, bankruptcy, loss mitigation, eviction, and Real Estate Owned ("REO") closings. FHFA-OIG audited FHFA's oversight of the RAN law firms' services in response to a Congressional request regarding potential abuses. FHFA-OIG found that FHFA had failed to strengthen its RAN oversight in a timely manner. For example, there were indicators as early as 2006 that could have led FHFA (and its predecessor) to identify the heightened risk posed by foreclosure processing abuses within Fannie Mae's default-related legal services network. Indicators such as a significant increase in foreclosures accompanying the deterioration of the housing market, consumer complaints alleging improper foreclosures, contemporaneous media reports of foreclosure abuses, and public court filings in Florida and elsewhere highlighting such abuses should have triggered careful assessment and action by FHFA. Notwithstanding these indicators, FHFA did not devote attention to this issue until August 2010.

FHFA-OIG recommended that FHFA: (1) review its failures to identify RAN foreclosure abuses earlier and improve its capacity to identify new and emerging risks; (2) implement comprehensive examination guidance and procedures together with supervisory plans for default-related legal services; and (3) implement policies and procedures to address poor performance by the Enterprises' default-related legal services vendors.

FHFA-OIG Office of Evaluations, Report No. EVL-2012-001: FHFA's Oversight of Troubled Federal Home Loan Banks (January 11, 2012)

Since 2008, four FHLBanks have faced significant financial and operational difficulties, primarily due to their investments in certain high-risk mortgage-backed securities. FHFA oversees the FHLBanks and recognizes the need to ensure that they do not abuse their GSE status and engage in imprudent activities. An FHFA-OIG evaluation identified several positive actions FHFA has taken regarding its oversight of the troubled FHLBanks, including encouraging fiscally conservative dividend and investment practices, and closely monitoring them through examinations and ongoing communications. However, the evaluation also found that FHFA has not taken critical steps to strengthen its oversight, including: (1) establishing a consistent and transparent written enforcement policy for troubled FHLBanks, which has contributed to instances where FHFA has not acted proactively to hold those troubled FHLBanks and their officers sufficiently accountable for engaging in questionable risk taking; (2) implementing an automated management information system that provides ready access to current information about the deficiencies identified in its examinations and the status of efforts to address them; and (3) consistently documenting substantive interactions with FHLBanks, including instances in which it has suggested that an FHLBank remove senior officers.

FHFA-OIG Office of Evaluations, Report No. EVL-2012-002: Evaluation of FHFA's Management of Legal Fees for Indemnified Executives (February 22, 2012)

Between 2004 and October 31, 2011, Fannie Mae paid out $99.4 million in legal expenses for the defense of three former senior executives in lawsuits, investigations, and administrative actions; the Enterprise paid considerable additional sums for other executives. Further, Freddie Mac has paid $10.2 million in legal defense costs for former senior executives since its conservatorship began. An FHFA-OIG evaluation found that on the one hand, FHFA is interested in avoiding potential losses and is thus motivated to defend vigorously ongoing lawsuits against the Enterprises. On the other hand, FHFA has an interest in controlling significant costs, particularly the tens of millions of dollars of payments made to attorneys and others involved in representing former senior executives. To their credit, Fannie Mae and Freddie Mac have taken steps to manage costs associated with lawsuits against their indemnification-eligible directors and officers. However, members of Congress and others have questioned the amount and appropriateness of these legal fee expenditures, especially given the federal government's very large federal investment in the Enterprises ($187.5 billion as of April 4, 2012). In light of these concerns, FHFA-OIG recommended that FHFA work to limit and control legal expenses to the extent possible and reasonable.

FHFA-OIG Office of Audits, Report No. AUD-2012-001: FHFA's Supervision of Freddie Mac's Controls over Mortgage Servicing Contractors (March 7, 2012)

The Enterprises provide liquidity for mortgage lending by purchasing mortgages from mortgage originators, which can then use the sale proceeds to make more loans. After an Enterprise buys a mortgage, it contracts with a mortgage servicer to collect mortgage payments, set aside taxes and insurance premiums in escrow, forward interest and principal payments to the contractually designated party, and respond to payment defaults. In late 2010, a federal interagency review of 14 large mortgage servicers found critical weaknesses in their foreclosure governance processes, foreclosure document preparation procedures, and oversight and monitoring of third-party vendors, including foreclosure attorneys. In light of these findings, FHFA-OIG initiated a performance audit to assess whether FHFA has an effective supervisory control structure and sufficient examination coverage and oversight activities to adequately and timely identify and mitigate risks involving mortgage servicing contractors. The audit covered FHFA's supervision of Freddie Mac.

FHFA-OIG found that FHFA and Freddie Mac have taken action to improve their oversight of mortgage servicing, but noted some areas in which FHFA could enhance its supervision of the Enterprises' controls over mortgage servicing contractors. FHFA had not clearly defined its own servicer oversight role, established comprehensive regulations and guidance for such oversight, adequately monitored servicer performance, adequately assessed the operational risks posed by Freddie Mac's servicing contractors, or sufficiently considered relevant findings by other federal agencies. In light of these control deficiencies, FHFA was not assured that the risk associated with Freddie Mac's servicing operations was being managed sufficiently.

FHFA-OIG recommended that the Agency: (1) establish and implement regulations or guidance for servicing oversight and risk management; (2) direct Freddie Mac to implement servicer performance metrics for a larger cross section of servicers to achieve additional credit loss savings; and (3) improve procedures for coordination with other federal agencies that oversee servicers. Although this audit focused on FHFA's supervision of Freddie Mac, the first and third recommendations are applicable to both Enterprises.

FHFA-OIG Office of Audits, Report No. AUD-2012-003: FHFA's Oversight of Fannie Mae's Single-Family Underwriting Standards (March 22, 2012)

An Enterprise will not purchase an originating lender's mortgage that does not satisfy the Enterprise's underwriting standards, unless the Enterprise approves a deviation ("variance"), which relaxes those standards. During the housing boom, variances contributed to Fannie Mae's credit losses and credit-related expenses, so FHFA-OIG audited FHFA's oversight of Fannie Mae's single-family mortgage underwriting standards and the internal controls over them. FHFA-OIG found that although FHFA has taken steps to ensure that mortgages purchased by the Enterprises conform to underwriting standards, the Agency's oversight of underwriting is limited, and it relies largely on the Enterprises to oversee and establish underwriting standards and to grant variances. FHFA-OIG concluded that the Agency can strengthen its oversight by: (1) creating formal processes for reviewing both the Enterprises' underwriting standards and variances from them; and (2) enhancing its guidance for planning and conducting its examinations of the Enterprises' underwriting quality control. FHFA-OIG reasoned that these steps could support not only the Enterprises' safe and sound operation, but also the preservation and conservation of Enterprise assets.

FHFA-OIG Office of Investigations, Investigation of Colonial Bank and TBW

FHFA-OIG has contributed significantly to the multi-agency investigation and prosecution of fraud involving Colonial Bank and the Taylor, Bean & Whitaker Mortgage Corporation ("TBW"), which had been one of the largest privately held mortgage lending companies in the United States. TBW originated, purchased, sold, and serviced residential mortgage loans, and also pooled loans that it originated as collateral for mortgage-backed securities guaranteed by Freddie Mac and by the Government National Mortgage Association ("Ginnie Mae"). Investigative efforts uncovered an extensive scheme within TBW's senior management to defraud the federal government as well as Freddie Mac, which included falsely inflating an account receivable balance for loan participations in TBW's financial statements. These falsified financial statements were subsequently provided to Freddie Mac and Ginnie Mae to support the renewal of TBW's authority to sell and service securities issued by them, causing Freddie Mac to suffer significant losses when TBW closed and filed for bankruptcy. To date, eight defendants have been convicted, seven of whom have also been found jointly and severally liable for a $3.5 billion restitution judgment. Further, seven TBW defendants have either been suspended and/or debarred from doing business with the federal government, or have debarment proceedings pending against them.

FHFA-OIG's investigation partners include the Office of the Special Inspector General for the Troubled Asset Relief Program ("SIGTARP"), the Federal Bureau of Investigation ("FBI"), the Office of Inspector General for the Federal Deposit Insurance Corporation, the Office of Inspector General for the Department of Housing and Urban Development ("HUD-OIG"), Internal Revenue Service ⊠ Criminal Investigation ("IRS-CI"), and the Securities and Exchange Commission. The Financial Crimes Enforcement Network ("FinCEN") also provided investigative support. The cases are being prosecuted by the Fraud Section of the Criminal Division at DOJ and the U.S. Attorney for the Eastern District of Virginia.

FHFA-OIG Office of Investigations, Investigation of Marshall Home and Margaret Broderick

On July 1, 2011, Marshall E. Home, of Tucson, Arizona, was arrested by FBI and FHFA-OIG Special Agents as a result of a criminal complaint filed in the U.S. District Court for the District of Arizona charging him with two counts of false claims in bankruptcy. He was indicted on these charges on July 13, 2011. Home and his wife, Margaret E. Broderick, were charged in a superseding indictment on September 7, 2011. Among other misdeeds, the defendants are alleged to have filed or caused to be filed before the U S. Bankruptcy Court 173 false claims, many involving mortgages guaranteed by the Enterprises. Home also allegedly registered the name "Federal National Mortgage Association" – Fannie Mae's official corporate name – with the Arizona Secretary of State as a trade name, then either filed or caused to be filed with county recorders deeds for real property owned by Fannie Mae. These deeds purported to transfer title from Fannie Mae to the "Independent Rights Party." The defendants also allegedly wrongfully transferred Freddie Mac properties, for a total of 28 wrongfully transferred properties collectively valued at over $8 million. These transfers interfered with the Enterprises' rights in those properties, causing them losses. This investigation is being conducted jointly by the FBI and FHFA-OIG.

FHFA-OIG Office of Investigations, Investigation of Home Owners Protection Economics, Inc.

On August 8, 2011, Christopher S. Godfrey, Dennis Fischer, Vernell Burris Jr., and Brian M. Kelly were arrested pursuant to a 20-count indictment unsealed in U.S. District Court for the District of Massachusetts that charged them with conspiracy, wire fraud, mail fraud, and misuse of a government seal. The indictment alleges that the defendants – all officers of Home Owners Protection Economics, Inc. ("HOPE"), a Florida company – and their employees used misrepresentations to entice financially distressed homeowners to pay HOPE an up-front fee in order to receive federally funded modifications to their mortgages, many of which were held or guaranteed by the Enterprises. One misrepresentation alleged by the indictment was the spurious claim that homeowners were virtually guaranteed, with HOPE's assistance, to receive a loan modification under the Treasury Department's Home Affordable Modification Program ("HAMP"), which Fannie Mae administered. HOPE is reported to have collected more than $3 million in fees from misled homeowners. This case is being jointly investigated with SIGTARP, IRS-CI, the U.S. Marshals Service, the Office of the Attorney General of Florida, the Palm Beach County Sheriff's Office, and the Delray Beach (FL) Police Department.

FHFA-OIG Office of Investigations, Investigation of Horizon Property Holdings/ Cydney Sanchez

On December 1, 2011, Horizon Property Holdings employees Jewel Hinkles (aka Cydney Sanchez), Bernadette Guidry, Jesse Wheeler, Cynthia Corn, and Brent Medearis were indicted on mail and bankruptcy fraud charges in the Eastern District of California. According to the indictment, from 2008 through at least February 2010, Horizon received at least $5 million in fees from homeowners facing foreclosure. The defendants allegedly told homeowners that for a substantial up-front payment and a monthly fee they would save the homeowners' residences from foreclosure. The indictment further alleges that contrary to the defendants' representations, they failed to arrange for the modification of the homeowners' mortgages. This is a joint investigation with the U.S. Postal Inspection Service, the FBI, and the Stanislaus County District Attorney's Office.

FHFA-OIG Office of Investigations, Investigation of Flahive Law Corporation

On March 8, 2012, Gregory Thomas Flahive, Cynthia Renee Flahive, and Michael Kent Johnson were charged in a California state court with grand theft and conspiracy for their role in a fraudulent loan modification scheme. FHFA-OIG, working with the San Joaquin Valley Mortgage Fraud Task Force, assisted the California Attorney General's Office and SIGTARP in this investigation.

FHFA-OIG's Planned Financial Oversight Work and Related Activities

- ### *Audit, Evaluation and Survey Plan*
  FHFA-OIG's Audit, Evaluation and Survey Plan focuses on those FHFA operations that can provide the greatest benefits or that pose the greatest risks to the Agency, Congress, and the public. In the financial oversight context, these include: (1) regulating and managing Enterprise conservatorships, including efforts to prevent foreclosures, mitigate losses, service mortgage loans, and manage and sell foreclosed properties; and (2) overseeing FHL Banks and their associated risks, including investment portfolio management and concentrations, credit underwriting, and administration.

- ### *Investigations Strategy*
  FHFA-OIG has numerous open investigations, some of which are being conducted with law enforcement partners. FHFA-OIG will continue to develop close working relationships with other federal, state, and local law enforcement agencies.

- ### *Hotline*
  FHFA-OIG's Hotline allows concerned parties to confidentially report information regarding possible fraud, waste, or abuse related to FHFA or the GSEs. FHFA-OIG honors all applicable whistleblower protections. FHFA-OIG promotes the Hotline through its website, posters, emails targeted to FHFA and GSE employees, and its Semiannual Reports to the Congress.

- ### *Regulatory Review*
  Consistent with the Inspector General Act, FHFA-OIG considers whether proposed legislation and regulations related to FHFA are efficient, economical, legal, and susceptible to fraud and abuse. FHFA-OIG makes recommendations to FHFA as necessary and monitors its compliance with recommended courses of action.

- ### *Coordinating with Other Oversight Organizations*
  FHFA-OIG actively participates in the Financial Fraud Enforcement Task Force ("FFETF"), a broad coalition of state and federal law enforcement agencies, prosecutors, and other entities. FHFA-OIG is a member of several FFETF task forces and working groups, including: (1) the Mortgage Fraud Working Group; (2) the Securities and Commodities Fraud Working Group; (3) the Residential Mortgage Backed Securities Working Group; and (4) the Recovery Act, Procurement, and Grant Fraud Working Group.

  FHFA-OIG spearheaded the creation of a new working group, the Federal Housing Inspectors General, which includes the Offices of Inspector General for federal agencies with primary responsibility for housing, including FHFA, HUD, the Department of Veterans Affairs, and the Department of Agriculture. In November 2011, the working group published the *Compendium of Federal Single Family Mortgage Programs and Related Activities*, which discusses the members' missions and activities and describes their agencies' single-family mortgage programs. The Federal Housing Inspectors General collaborate on multiple joint initiatives.

FHFA-OIG actively participates in the Council of the Inspectors General on Integrity and Efficiency ("CIGIE"). The Inspector General serves on CIGIE's Inspection and Evaluation Committee, which supports and promotes evaluation and inspection practice in the OIG community. The Inspector General also serves as vice chairman of CIGIE's Suspension and Debarment Working Group, which is charged with improving the effectiveness of federal suspension and debarment practices.

FHFA-OIG has also partnered with FinCEN, SIGTARP, HUD-OIG, the FBI, and the Secret Service to share data, analyze internal complaints, and identify trends. Doing so allows the partnering entities to leverage their combined investigative resources on identifying, investigating, and prosecuting those involved in fraud and other illegal activities related to their respective statutory authorities.

Audit, Evaluation and Survey Plan

FHFA-OIG's Audit, Evaluation and Survey Plan focuses on those FHFA operations that can provide the greatest benefits or that pose the greatest risks to the Agency, Congress, and the public. In the financial oversight context, these include: (1) regulating and managing Enterprise conservatorships, including efforts to prevent foreclosures, mitigate losses, service mortgage loans, and manage and sell foreclosed properties; and (2) overseeing FHLBanks and their associated risks, including investment portfolio management and concentrations, credit underwriting, and administration.

Investigations Strategy

FHFA-OIG has numerous open investigations, some of which are being conducted with law enforcement partners. FHFA-OIG will continue to develop close working relationships with other federal, state, and local law enforcement agencies.

Hotline

FHFA-OIG's Hotline allows concerned parties to confidentially report information regarding possible fraud, waste, or abuse related to FHFA or the GSEs. FHFA-OIG honors all applicable whistleblower protections. FHFA-OIG promotes the Hotline through its website, posters, emails targeted to FHFA and GSE employees, and its Semiannual Reports to the Congress.

Regulatory Review

Consistent with the Inspector General Act, FHFA-OIG considers whether proposed legislation and regulations related to FHFA are efficient, economical, legal, and susceptible to fraud and abuse. FHFA-OIG makes recommendations to FHFA as necessary and monitors its compliance with recommended courses of action.

Coordinating with Other Oversight Organizations

FHFA-OIG actively participates in the Financial Fraud Enforcement Task Force ("FFETF"), a broad coalition of state and federal law enforcement agencies, prosecutors, and other entities. FHFA-OIG is a member of several FFETF task forces and working groups, including: (1) the Mortgage Fraud Working Group; (2) the Securities and Commodities Fraud Working Group; (3) the Residential Mortgage Backed Securities Working Group; and (4) the Recovery Act, Procurement, and Grant Fraud Working Group.

FHFA-OIG spearheaded the creation of a new working group, the Federal Housing Inspectors General, which includes the Offices of Inspector General for federal agencies with primary responsibility for housing, including FHFA, HUD, the Department of Veterans Affairs, and the Department of Agriculture. In November 2011, the working group published the *Compendium of Federal Single Family Mortgage Programs and Related Activities,* which discusses the members' missions and activities and describes their agencies' single-family mortgage programs. The Federal Housing Inspectors General collaborate on multiple joint initiatives.

FHFA-OIG actively participates in the Council of the Inspectors General on Integrity and Efficiency ("CIGIE"). The Inspector General serves on CIGIE's Inspection and Evaluation Committee, which supports and promotes evaluation and inspection practice in the OIG community. The Inspector General also serves as vice chairman of CIGIE's Suspension and Debarment Working Group, which is charged with improving the effectiveness of federal suspension and debarment practices.

FHFA-OIG has also partnered with FinCEN, SIGTARP, HUD-OIG, the FBI, and the Secret Service to share data, analyze internal complaints, and identify trends. Doing so allows the partnering entities to leverage their combined investigative resources on identifying, investigating, and prosecuting those involved in fraud and other illegal activities related to their respective statutory authorities.

Office of Inspector General
National Credit Union Administration

Agency Overview

The National Credit Union Administration (NCUA) is responsible for chartering, insuring, and supervising Federal credit unions and administering the National Credit Union Share Insurance Fund (NCUSIF). The NCUA also manages the Temporary Corporate Credit Union Stabilization Fund (TCCUSF),[4] the Community Development Revolving Loan Fund (CDRLF),[5] and the Central Liquidity Facility (CLF).[6]

Credit unions are member-owned, not-for-profit cooperative financial institutions formed to permit members to save, borrow, and obtain related financial services. NCUA charters and supervises federal credit unions, and insures accounts in federal and most state-chartered credit unions across the country through the NCUSIF, a federal fund backed by the full faith and credit of the United States government.

Major NCUA Programs

Supervision

NCUA's supervision program contributes to the safety and soundness of the credit union system. Identifying and resolving risk concerns such as credit risk, concentration risk, and strategic risk continue to be the primary focus of the program. NCUA supervises natural person credit unions through annual examinations, regulatory enforcement, providing guidance in regulations and Letters to Credit Unions, and taking administrative actions as necessary to manage credit union risk.

NCUA also supervises corporate credit unions through examinations and other actions to ensure that the corporates' ongoing operations effectively meet the needs of the natural person credit unions they service. As part of the Corporate System Resolution, the NCUA Board uses the TCCUSF to pay the costs associated with stabilizing and resolving the corporate credit union system.

Insurance

The NCUA administers the NCUSIF, which provides insurance for deposits held at federally-insured natural person and corporate credit unions nationwide. The fund is capitalized by credit unions. NCUA manages the fund to ensure members' deposits are insured. In 2010, Congress permanently increased the insurance limit from $100,000 to $250,000 per depositor.

Small Credit Union Initiatives

---

4   The TCCUSF was established as a revolving fund in the U.S. Treasury under the management of the NCUA Board. The purposes of the TCCUSF are to accrue the losses of the corporate credit union system and, over time, assess the credit union system for the recovery of such losses.

5   The NCUA's CDRLF, which was established by Congress, makes loans and Technical Assistance Grants to low-income designated credit unions.

6   The CLF is a mixed-ownership government corporation the purpose of which is to supply emergency loans to member credit unions.

The NCUA fosters credit union development, particularly the expansion of services provided by small credit unions to eligible consumers. NCUA fulfills this goal through training, partnerships and assistance. A major source of assistance is the CDRLF, which provides loans and grants to credit unions which serve low-income customers. CDRLF assistance enables these credit unions to provide basic financial services and stimulate economic activities in their communities.

Consumer Protection

NCUA protects credit union members through effective enforcement of consumer protection regulations and requirements. NCUA's Office of Consumer Protection (OCP), created in 2010, is responsible for consumer protection in the areas of fair lending examinations, member complaints, and financial literacy. It is also responsible for chartering, field of membership expansions, by-law amendments, and other charter-related functions.

Asset Management

The NCUA's Asset Management and Assistance Center (AMAC) conducts credit union liquidations and performs management and recovery of assets. AMAC assists NCUA regional offices with the review of large, complex loan portfolios and actual or potential bond claims. AMAC also participates extensively in the operational phases of conservatorships and records reconstruction. AMAC's purpose is to minimize costs to the NCUSIF and to credit union members.

Office of Minority and Women Inclusion

NCUA formed the Office of Minority and Women Inclusion (OMWI) in response to the *"Dodd-Frank Wall Street Reform and Consumer Protection Act of 2010"* (Dodd-Frank). OMWI has the responsibility for ensuring compliance with Dodd-Frank in the areas of diversity, civil rights and the promotion of minority and women hiring and contracting practices throughout the credit union industry.

The NCUA Office of Inspector General

The 1988 amendments to the *Inspector General Act of 1978* (IG Act), 5 U.S.C. App. 3, established IGs in 33 designated Federal entities (DFEs), including the NCUA.[7] The NCUA Office of Inspector General (OIG) was established in 1989. The NCUA IG is appointed by, reports to, and is under the general supervision of, a three-member presidentially-appointed Board. The OIG staff consists of nine FTEs: the IG, the Deputy IG, the Counsel to the IG; the Director of Investigations, four senior auditors, and an office manager. The OIG promotes the economy, efficiency, and effectiveness of NCUA programs and operations, and detects and deters fraud, waste and abuse, thereby supporting the NCUA's mission of facilitating the availability of credit union services to all eligible consumers through a regulatory environment that fosters a safe and sound credit union system. The OIG supports this mission by conducting independent audits, investigations, and other activities, and by keeping the NCUA Board and the Congress fully and currently informed of its work.

---

7   5 U.S.C. App. 3, §8G.

The OIG Role in Financial Oversight

The *"Dodd-Frank Wall Street Reform and Consumer Protection Act"* fundamentally altered the regulatory and financial services landscape. Since the inception of the financial crisis and the passage of Dodd-Frank, the NCUA has worked to address a wide set of concerns about the regulatory regime that Dodd-Frank aimed to change. In its 2011 annual report, the Financial Stability Oversight Council (FSOC) made recommendations to fulfill Dodd-Frank's mandates which included: (1) heightened risk management and supervisory attention in specific areas; (2) further reforms to address structural vulnerabilities in key markets; (3) steps to address reform of the housing finance market; and (4) coordination on financial regulatory reform. These broad recommendations form the outline of depository regulatory reform over the coming years. NCUA has set goals to address those recommendations in a manner tailored to credit unions, at the least cost, and in the most targeted manner. The OIG continues to monitor closely the agency's efforts to achieve those goals.

OIG Capping Report on Material Loss Reviews

In many cases, the agency was already working to address the FSOC's recommendations as a result of OIG findings and recommendations as set forth in audit and Material Loss Review (MLR)[8] reports and, in particular, findings and recommendations summarized in the "OIG Capping Report on Material Loss Reviews," Report #OIG-10-20, issued on November 23, 2010[9]. The Capping Report summarized significant findings from MLRs the OIG conducted and made 11 recommendations to NCUA management for corrective action. Issues discussed in the Capping Report's findings and recommendations related to the examination and supervision procedures for overseeing credit unions and included documentation, monitoring, ratings, call reports, third party relationships, due diligence, exam procedures, quality control reviews, and regulatory guidance.

In a letter dated April 24, 2012, the NCUA OIG reported to Representative Darrell Issa, Chairman, Committee on Oversight and Government Reform, that it is continuing to monitor the NCUA's action plans to address the following three most significant open and unimplemented OIG audit recommendations:[10]

1. Determine whether to propose and/or change regulatory guidance to establish limits or other controls for concentrations that pose an unacceptable safety and soundness risk and determine an appropriate range of examiner response to high risk concentrations.

2. Re-emphasize examination guidance for third-party relationships, with particular attention to the assessment of the risk the relationship may pose to the credit union's safety and soundness.

---

8   The Federal Credit Union Act (FCUA), 12 U.S.C. 1790d(j), requires that the OIG conduct a MLR when the NCUSIF has incurred a material loss with respect to a credit union. A material loss is defined as (1) exceeding the sum of $25 million and (2) an amount equal to 10% of the total assets of the credit union at the time at which the Board initiated assistance or was appointed liquidating agent.
Dodd-Frank amended the FCUA to further require the OIG to (1) perform limited reviews of all credit union losses under the $25 million threshold to assess whether an in-depth review (consistent with the scope of a MLR) is warranted; and (2) report to the NCUA Board and the Congress every six months on: (a) the results of the limited reviews; and (b) the timeframe for performing any in-depth reviews the OIG determines should be subsequently conducted.

9   *http://www.ncua.gov/about/Leadership/CO/OIG/Documents/OIG201020CappRpt.pdf*

10   All three of these open and unimplemented recommendations were set forth in the Capping Report.

---

3. Require a documented secondary review of the final CAMEL ratings by the Supervisory Examiner for all credit unions over $100 million in assets prior to issuance to credit union management.

With regard to the first recommendation, NCUA agreed with the OIG and has provided training to examiners and issued a Supervisory Letter to credit unions advising them how to evaluate and manage concentration risk. NCUA further anticipates—by the end of 2012—finalizing revisions to its current Prompt Corrective Action (PCA) regulation to place additional emphasis on the various concentrations of credit on a balance sheet and base minimum net worth levels in association with concentrations.

NCUA also agreed to and is responding to the OIG's recommendation that the agency place renewed emphasis on examination guidance for third-party relationships, with particular attention to the assessment of the risk those relationships may pose to the credit union's safety and soundness. Specifically, the agency has provided training to examiners and issued nine Letters to Credit Unions and Supervisory Letters over the past several years. Currently, NCUA is working on enhancing the examination and supervision program for oversight of Credit Union Service Organizations (CUSO), as well as revising the CUSO regulation. Again, the agency expects to complete these efforts by year end 2012.

Finally, in response to the recommendation that NCUA require a documented secondary review of the final CAMEL ratings by the Supervisory Examiner for all credit unions with over $100 million in assets prior to issuance to credit union management, the agency revised its National Supervision Policy Manual to address this issue and is currently working on a soft rollout. Implementation of the new policy began in May 2012.

Interest Rate Risk Rule

In recommending that agencies heighten risk management and supervisory attention, the FSOC further advised agencies to bolster resilience to unexpected interest rate shifts. Likewise, several of the MLRs the OIG conducted over the past several years noted that credit unions without an appropriate interest rate risk (IRR) policy, and a program to effectively implement that policy as part of their asset liability management responsibilities, caused losses to the NCUSIF and/or contributed to the credit union's failure.[11] These MLRs further identified where improvements could be made in NCUA's monitoring of IRR.

In January, 2012, the NCUA Board adopted a final amendment to the agency's insurance rules requiring certain federally-insured credit unions to have a written policy to address IRR management as well as an effective IRR program for successful asset liability management.[12] To assist credit unions, the final rule includes an appendix setting forth guidance on developing an IRR policy, and effectively implementing a program based on generally recognized best practices for safely and soundly managing interest rate risk. NCUA tailored the final IRR rule to apply to credit unions at most risk for interest rate shocks. As a result, the final rule will not apply to credit unions with less than $10 million in assets. Federally-insured credit unions

---

[11] The term "interest rate risk" refers to the vulnerability of a credit union's financial condition to adverse movements in market interest rates. For example, changes to a credit union's funding costs generally are considered part of the inherent rate risk associated with a fixed-rate mortgage loan. A borrower with a fixed-rate mortgage loan is unaffected by increases in market interest rates because his payment is based on a "fixed" rate. The credit union that originated the mortgage loan, however, is subject to losses in the market value of these mortgages from the increases in the market interest rates. Furthermore, as market interest rates rise, there is a concomitant increase in the credit union's funding costs, or the interest rate the credit union pays on the money it uses to "fund" the mortgage loan.

[12] http://www.ncua.gov/Legal/Documents/Regulations/FIR20120126InterestRateRiskProg.pdf

with assets between $10 million and $50 million must have a written policy if first mortgage loans plus total investments longer than five years is equal to or greater than 100 percent of net worth. Federally-insured credit unions with assets more than $50 million must comply with the new IRR rule.

The new rule gives affected credit unions until September 30, 2012, to comply.

Audit of NCUA's Small Credit Union Supervision Program and Credit Union Examination Appeal Process

By letter dated February 10, 2012, Senator Tim Johnson, Chairman of the Senate Banking Committee, requested-- under the aegis of Dodd-Frank and its mandate that federal agencies improve oversight of the financial systems they regulate--that the NCUA OIG conduct an audit of NCUA's small credit union supervision program, including examination timelines and how NCUA ensures consistency in the administration of examinations nation-wide.[13]   Chairman Johnson requested further that NCUA report on the ability of federally-regulated credit unions to question examination results, such as through an Ombudsman, an appeals process, or informal channels, and the frequency of such appeals. Chairman Johnson's request comes at a time when two proposed bills, S. 2160 and H.R. 3461, both entitled *"Financial Institutions Examination Fairness and Reform Act,"* would codify financial institution examination standards and move the appeals process outside the agencies.

The OIG has initiated an audit in response to the Chairman's request. The expected completion date is August 2012.

Loan Participation Rule

In December 2011, the NCUA published a proposed rule with a request for comment that would extend safety and soundness protections on loan participations to all federally insured credit unions.[14] The proposed rule change followed an OIG review, in mid-2010, involving a loan participation program at several credit unions nation-wide, where the originator was not the credit union. Because of resulting safety and soundness concerns at one of the credit unions, the OIG conducted a review of a third-party's involvement in the loan participation program and the agency's oversight of it. The proposed rule addresses the concerns the OIG review identified.

Under the proposed rule, non-federal credit union originators would be required to retain 10% of the original loan risk. The rule also requires that (1) underwriting standards for loan participations meet or exceed the underwriting standards that each purchasing credit union uses for originating their own loans; (2) credit unions buying participation interests establish parameters for reviewing loan documentation; and (3) credit unions perform on-going due diligence on purchased loans.

Further, the proposed rule provides that (1) buyers would be protected from acquiring undue concentrations; (2) loan participations purchased from one originating lender could not exceed 25% of net worth; (3)

---

13   Chairman Johnson's letter was sent collectively to each of the Inspectors General at the Federal Reserve Board, the Department of the Treasury, the Federal Deposit Insurance Corporation, and the NCUA. The letter requested that each agency conduct a separate audit and provide individual reports.

14   *http://www.ncua.gov/Legal/Documents/Regulations/PR20111222LoanParticipationsEtAl.pdf*

participation loans to one borrower could not exceed 15% of net worth; and (4) credit unions could apply to NCUA Regional Directors for waivers of these limits.

The rule is expected to be finalized in late 2012

Review of NCUA's Controls over Sensitive and Proprietary Information

Dodd-Frank created the CIGFO in part, to evaluate the effectiveness and internal operations of the FSOC. On December 8, 2011, CIGFO members approved a proposal to convene a working group to review FSOC's control of sensitive and proprietary information. The NCUA OIG conducted a review - concurrently with reviews by the other CIGFO members - in support of the CIGFO's "Audit of the Financial Stability Oversight Council's Controls over Sensitive and Proprietary Information." The results from the OIG's report will be incorporated into the CIGFO final report.

The objective was to review NCUA's policies, procedures, and practices for ensuring that FSOC-related information which the agency collects, shares, or deliberates is adequately protected from unauthorized disclosure. The report found that NCUA's existing policies and procedures are not sufficiently comprehensive to assist the agency in protecting confidential, non-public FSOC information, which it collects, shares, or deliberates, from unauthorized disclosure. Specifically, the OIG found that NCUA needs to improve its policies and procedures to address:

- Protecting oral communication of confidential non-public FSOC information;

- Inventorying or tracking FSOC information requests/responses;

- Controlling access to and authorizing release of confidential non-public information to FSOC, FSOC member agencies or other external parties (e.g., Congress);

- Marking FSOC information;

- A central person/group to coordinate all FSOC communications;

- Selecting, identifying, maintaining, and communicating to FSOC and its member agencies who the NCUA representatives are and their respective responsibilities;

- Identifying, controlling, and monitoring who within NCUA will have access to an who has accessed specific FSOC information and systems;

- Handling, controlling, and protecting FSOC information during teleconferences and telework sessions; and

- Consequences for the breach/unauthorized disclosure of FSOC information

The OIG is currently working on a separate report of its findings and observations that it will issue to NCUA management.

Office of Inspector General
United States Securities and Exchange Commission

Agency Overview

The mission of the United States Securities and Exchange Commission (SEC or Commission) is to protect investors; maintain fair, orderly, and efficient markets; and facilitate capital formation. The SEC strives to promote a market environment that is worthy of the public's trust and characterized by transparency and integrity. The SEC's core values consist of integrity, accountability, effectiveness, teamwork, fairness, and commitment to excellence. The SEC's goals are to foster and enforce compliance with the federal securities laws; establish an effective regulatory environment; facilitate access to the information investors need to make informed investment decisions; and enhance the Commission's performance through effective alignment and management of human resources, information, and financial capital.

SEC staff monitor and regulate a securities industry consisting of more than 35,000 registrants, including over 10,000 public companies, about 11,000 investment advisers, about 7,500 mutual funds, and about 5,000 broker-dealers, as well as national securities exchanges and self-regulatory organizations, 500 transfer agents, 15 national securities exchanges, 9 clearing agencies, 10 credit rating agencies, and alternate trading systems. Additionally, the agency has oversight responsibility for the Securities Investor Protection Corporation, the Financial Industry Regulatory Authority, the Municipal Securities Rulemaking Board, and the Public Company Accounting Oversight Board.

The SEC is organized into five main divisions—Corporation Finance; Enforcement; Investment Management; Trading and Markets; and Risk, Strategy, and Financial Innovation (RiskFin)—and 16 functional offices. The Commission has its headquarters in Washington, D.C., and has 11 regional offices located throughout the country. As of September 30, 2011, the SEC had 3,844 full-time equivalent employees, consisting of 3,806 permanent and 38 temporary full-time equivalent employees.

Mission of the SEC OIG

The role of the SEC Office of Inspector General (OIG) is to promote the integrity, efficiency, and effectiveness of the critical programs and operations of the SEC. This mission is best achieved by having an effective, vigorous, and independent office of seasoned and talented professionals who perform the following functions:

- conducting independent and objective audits, evaluations, investigations, and other reviews of SEC programs and operations;

- preventing and detecting fraud, waste, abuse, and mismanagement in SEC programs and operations;

- identifying vulnerabilities in SEC systems and operations and recommending constructive solutions;

- offering expert assistance to improve SEC programs and operations;

- communicating timely and useful information that facilitates management decision making and the achievement of measurable gains; and

- keeping the Commission and Congress fully and currently informed of significant issues and developments.

Acting Inspector General Noelle Maloney joined the SEC OIG as Deputy Inspector General in July 2008 and was named Acting Inspector General in January 2011. Since last year, the SEC OIG's Office of Audits has issued detailed assessments and reviews discussing issues critical to SEC operations and to the investing public and has made significant recommendations for improvement. Examples of work performed by the SEC OIG concerning financial oversight activities are described in detail below.

Recent Examples of Oversight Work Performed by the SEC OIG

Report of Review of Economic Analyses Performed by the Securities and Exchange Commission in Connection With Dodd-Frank Act Rulemakings

The Dodd-Frank Act added significantly to the SEC's workload by requiring that the Commission promulgate more than 100 new rules, create five new offices, and produce more than 20 studies and reports. It also gave the SEC considerable new responsibilities that will significantly affect the Commission's workload over the long term, including oversight of the over-the-counter derivatives market and hedge fund advisers; registration of municipal advisors and security-based swap market participants; enhanced supervision of Nationally Recognized Statistical Rating Organizations and clearing agencies; heightened regulation of asset-backed securities; and creation of a new whistleblower program.

In a February 15, 2011, letter, some members of the U.S. Senate Committee on Banking, Housing, and Urban Affairs (Senate Banking Committee) expressed concerns about the economic analyses and cost-benefit assessments being performed by federal financial regulatory agencies for certain rules required under Dodd-Frank. Specifically, these senators stated that they had received comments from members of the public who had performed their own analyses of the rules and identified flaws in the federal financial regulatory agencies' analyses.

On May 4, 2011, the SEC OIG received a formal letter signed by 10 members of the Senate Banking Committee requesting that the Inspectors General of the SEC, the Commodity Futures Trading Commission, the Federal Deposit Insurance Corporation, and the Federal Reserve initiate a review of the economic analyses performed by their respective agencies in connection with rulemaking initiatives under the Dodd-Frank Act. The letter asked that the SEC OIG review focus specifically on the cost-benefit analyses for the following Dodd-Frank Act regulatory initiatives:

- Credit Risk Retention, 76 Fed. Reg. 24090 (April 29, 2011)

- Clearing Agency Standards for Operation and Governance, 76 Fed. Reg. 14472 (March 16, 2011)

- Registration and Regulation of Security-Based Swap Execution Facilities, 76 Fed. Reg. 10948 (February 28, 2011)

- Reporting by Investment Advisers to Private Funds and Certain Commodity Pool Operators and Commodity Trading Advisors on Form PF, 76 Fed. Reg. 8068 (February 11, 2011)

- Registration of Municipal Advisors, 76 Fed. Reg. 824 (January 6, 2011)

- Conflict Minerals, 75 Fed. Reg. 80948 (December 23, 2010)

The OIG retained a technical expert to assist with its review of the SEC's economic or cost-benefit analyses in connection with Dodd-Frank Act rulemakings. On June 13, 2011, the SEC OIG responded to the Senate Banking Committee's request for review of SEC-conducted economic analyses.

The OIG review concluded that the SEC had conducted a systematic cost-benefit analysis for each of the six rules reviewed. Overall, the OIG found that the SEC formed teams with sufficient expertise to conduct a comprehensive and thoughtful economic analysis for each of the rulemakings. In several cases, the OIG found that RiskFin staff were involved early in the process and contributed extensively to the scope and breadth of the analyses. In these instances particularly, the OIG found that the analyses were thorough and had incorporated all aspects of the principles of the applicable Executive Orders and of the SEC's internal compliance handbook.

However, the OIG found that RiskFin's level of involvement in the cost-benefit analysis process varied considerably from rulemaking to rulemaking and that RiskFin had a stronger working relationship with some rulemaking teams than with others. The OIG's technical expert noted that it is critically important for RiskFin to be an integral part of the process because performing a cost-benefit analysis is fundamentally an exercise in economics and, according to the technical expert, RiskFin employees have a broader and deeper expertise in economics than employees outside of RiskFin.

In addition, the OIG identified two areas of potential deficiencies in the SEC's cost-benefit analyses: (1) the lack of macro-level analysis in the proposed release enumerating standards for clearing agency operation and governance and (2), the lack of quantitative assessment of the impact of proposed rules, particularly in connection with the requirement that municipal advisors register with the Commission. In the report on this review, the OIG stated its intention to further analyze these areas and issue a report on the results of the follow-up analysis. The OIG's full report on this initial review is available on the SEC's website at http://www.sec-oig.gov/Reports/AuditsInspections/2011/Report_6_13_11.pdf.

Follow-Up Review of Cost-Benefit Analyses in Selected SEC Dodd-Frank Act Rulemakings

On January 27, 2012, the OIG issued a report on its follow-up review of cost-benefit analyses in Dodd-Frank Act rulemakings. The follow-up review consisted of further examination of the SEC's economic analysis for a sample of Dodd-Frank Act rulemakings to determine whether the SEC's cost-benefit analyses for the rulemakings were in compliance with applicable federal requirements.

This follow-up review examined the economic analyses performed by the SEC in connection with the following five Dodd-Frank Act rulemakings:

- Shareholder Approval of Executive Compensation and Golden Parachute Compensation, 76 Fed. Reg. 6010 (Jan. 25, 2011)

- Disclosure for Asset-Backed Securities Required by Section 943 of the Dodd-Frank Wall Street Reform and Consumer Protection Act, 76 Fed. Reg. 4489 (Jan. 20, 2011)

- Issuer Review of Assets in Offerings of Asset-Backed Securities, 76 Fed. Reg. 4231 (Jan. 20, 2011)

- Reporting of Security-Based Swap Transaction Data, 75 Fed. Reg. 64643 (interim final temporary rule, Oct. 13, 2010)

- Regulation SBSR—Reporting and Dissemination of Security-Based Swap Information, 75 Fed. Reg. 75208 (proposed Nov. 19, 2010)

For this work, as for the initial review discussed above, the OIG retained a technical expert to assist with its review of the cost-benefit analyses. The follow-up review concluded that SEC rulemaking teams consistently adhered to internal policies for preparing cost-benefit analyses and followed a systematic process from inception to completion. Nonetheless, the OIG found that the extent of quantitative discussion in the cost-benefit analyses varied among rulemakings and that none of the analyses examined in the follow-up review attempted to quantify either benefits or costs other than information collection costs as required by federal regulation. In addition, the technical expert noted the crucial role that economists play in ensuring that cost-benefit analyses incorporate both qualitative and quantitative information.

Significantly, the OIG also found that the SEC's cost-benefit analyses for Dodd-Frank Act rulemakings generally focused on discretionary components—portions of rulemakings in which the Commission is able to exercise choice. The technical expert opined that in addition to satisfying statutory requirements, a cost-benefit analysis is intended to inform the public and other parts of government, including Congress, of the effects of alternative regulatory actions. Therefore, to the extent that the SEC performs cost-benefit analyses only for discretionary rulemaking activities, according to the technical expert, the SEC may not be fulfilling the essential purposes of such analyses—providing a full picture of whether the benefits of a regulatory action are likely to justify its costs and discovering which regulatory alternatives would be the most cost-effective.

In addition, based on examination of several Dodd-Frank Act rulemakings, the OIG found that the SEC sometimes used multiple baselines in its cost-benefit analyses that were ambiguous or internally inconsistent. For example, in the SEC's interim final temporary rule for registration of municipal advisors, portions of the cost-benefit analysis assumed as a baseline a minimal registration process that would allow municipal advisors to continue their usual activities with limited disruption. However, other parts of the cost-benefit analysis assumed that municipal advisers would be required to cease their advisory activities in the absence of a registration process, resulting in a shutdown of the municipal advisory market. The review also found that there was often considerable overlap between the cost-benefit analyses and the efficiency, competition, and capital formation sections of the releases for Dodd-Frank Act regulations, and that redundancy could be reduced by combining these two sections.

The follow-up review also found that some SEC Dodd-Frank Act rulemakings lacked clear, explicit explanations of the justification for regulatory action. Specifically, some of the rulemakings that were premised on market failure alluded to market failure but did not explicitly cite it as a justification or fully discuss it.

Other rulemakings included language that erroneously suggested a market failure justification and contained no compelling alternative rationale in support of the action. OMB Circular A-4, Regulatory Analysis, identifies market failure as one of several possible justifications for federal agency regulation. According to the OIG's technical expert, a more focused discussion of market failure in cost-benefit analyses would lay out the rationale for regulation more clearly to Congress, the general public, and the SEC itself.

Finally, the follow-up review found that although some of the SEC's Dodd-Frank Act rulemakings may result in significant costs or benefits to the Commission itself, internal costs and benefits were rarely addressed in the cost-benefit analyses. According to the OIG's technical expert, considering internal administrative costs and benefits is consistent with the purposes of a cost-benefit analysis and provides a more complete picture of economic costs and benefits associated with government regulation.

Based on the results of the follow-up review, the OIG made the following recommendations:

1. SEC rulewriting divisions and RiskFin should consider ways for economists to provide additional input into cost-benefit analyses of SEC rulemakings to assist in including both quantitative and qualitative information to the extent possible.

2. The Office of the General Counsel, in consultation with RiskFin, should reconsider its guidance that the SEC should perform economic analyses for rulemaking activities to the extent that the SEC exercises discretion and should consider whether a pre-statute baseline should be used whenever possible.

3. SEC rulemaking teams should generally use a single, consistent baseline in the cost-benefit analyses of their rulemakings related to a particular topic. The baseline being used should be specified at the beginning of the cost-benefit analysis section. If multiple baselines are appropriate, such as for evaluating alternative approaches or explaining the SEC's use of discretion, they should also be explained and justified.

4. SEC rulewriting divisions should consider discontinuing the practice of drafting separate cost-benefit analysis and efficiency, competition, and capital formation sections and instead provide a more integrated discussion of these issues in rule releases.

5. The Commission should consider directing rulemaking teams to (a) explicitly discuss market failure as a justification for regulatory action in the cost-benefit analysis of each rule that is based in whole or in part on perceived market failure or (b) in the absence of market failure, demonstrate a compelling social purpose that justifies regulatory action.

6. SEC rulemaking teams should consider including internal costs and benefits in the cost-benefit analyses of rulemakings.

The OIG's full report is available on the SEC's website at http://www.sec-oig.gov/Reports/AuditsInspections/2012/499.pdf.

Establishment of the Office of Minority and Women Inclusion

On February 10, 2011, the SEC Inspector General testified before the Subcommittee on Financial Services and General Government, Committee on Appropriations, U.S. House of Representatives, concerning his oversight of the SEC by means of the OIG's audit and investigative functions. During that testimony, Congresswoman Barbara Lee (D-California) asked about the status of the SEC's efforts in creating the office of Minority and Women Inclusion. In response to Congresswoman Lee's request, the OIG researched the SEC's implementation of the requirement for an Office of Minority and Women Inclusion and provided Congresswoman Lee with a copy of the OIG's report.

The OIG determined that the SEC did not establish an Office of Minority and Women Inclusion within six months after the date of enactment of the Dodd-Frank Act, as required by section 342(a)(1)(A) of the act. SEC management informed the OIG that it did not meet this deadline because Congress had not yet acted on the Commission's request that Congress approve creation of the office. SEC management further indicated that, in the meantime, the SEC organized a planning group to discuss and address issues related to the establishment of the office, and the SEC's Office of Administrative Services and Office of Equal Employment Opportunity were conducting activities intended to promote minority and women inclusion in SEC contracts and hiring. The full report is available on the OIG website at http://www.sec-oig.gov/Reports/AuditsInspections/2011/496.pdf.

Other Planned Oversight Work

The OIG plans to perform other audit work in connection with its oversight of the SEC and concerns as they apply to the broader financial system.

Audit of the SEC's Tips, Complaints, and Referrals Process

The SEC typically receives thousands of tips complaints and referrals (TCRs) every year from investors and the general public, as well as from broker-dealers, investment advisers, self-regulatory organizations, other government agencies, and foreign regulators. Different divisions and offices located throughout the SEC's Washington, D.C., headquarters, as well as the SEC's eleven regional offices, receive TCRs. These communications come in through a variety of means, including web forms, e-mail, phone calls, regular mail and personal interactions by staff.

As part of its mission to protect investors and ensure market integrity and in response to certain deficiencies identified and recommendations made in previous OIG reports, the SEC conducted a comprehensive review of its processes for receiving, recording, tracking, and taking action on TCRs. The review resulted in a comprehensive improvement plan, including the SEC's TCR policies, processes, and information technology systems. As part of that improvement plan, in March 2011, the SEC issued a new internal policy setting forth the responsibilities of all SEC staff regarding the intake of TCRs and implement a temporary TCR repository. Thereafter, the SEC designed and implemented a new system to enable the SEC to gather TCRs and support the internal business process to review, analyze, qualify, and report on the information submitted.

During Congressional testimony by the former SEC Inspector General in February 2011, members of the Financial Services and General Government Subcommittee of the House of Representatives Committee on Appropriations expressed interest in ensuring that the SEC's new TCR system is functioning efficiently and effectively and has remedied problems that occurred in the past. In response, the former Inspector General informed the Subcommittee members that once the new TCR system had been functioning for a sufficient period of time, the OIG would conduct a careful review of the system. Accordingly, the OIG is in the process of conducting an audit that examines the SEC's TCR system. The specific objectives of the audit are (1) to assess whether the SEC receives, records, tracks and escalates TCR items in accordance with internal policies and procedures, laws, and regulations; (2) test the accuracy and completeness of data and reports generated from the TCR system; and (3) review the controls and procedures utilized to ensure the accuracy and completeness of the transfer of information from the interim TCR repository to the new TCR system.

Study of Whistleblower Protections Established Under the Dodd-Frank Act

Section 922(d)(1) of the Dodd Frank-Act requires that the SEC OIG conduct a study of the whistleblower protections established under the act. The study is to address, among other things, whether the final rules and regulations issued under section 922 have made the SEC's whistleblower protection program clearly defined and user friendly; whether the program is promoted on the SEC's website and has been widely publicized; whether the Commission is prompt in responding to information provided by whistleblowers and applications for awards filed by whistleblowers, updating whistleblowers about the status of their applications, and otherwise communicating with the interested parties; and whether reward levels are adequate to entice whistleblowers to provide information or so high that they encourage illegitimate claims. The Dodd-Frank Act requires that the study be completed no later than January 2013.

Office of the Special Inspector General for the Troubled Asset Relief Program

Background

The Office of the Special Inspector General for the Troubled Asset Relief Program ("SIGTARP") was established by Section 121 of the Emergency Economic Stabilization Act of 2008 ("EESA"). Under EESA, the Special Inspector General has the duty, among other things, to conduct, supervise, and coordinate audits and investigations of the purchase, management, and sale of assets under the Troubled Asset Relief Program ("TARP") or as deemed appropriate by the Special Inspector General.

TARP will continue to exist for years. TARP programs that support the housing market and certain securities markets are scheduled to last until at least 2018. Treasury cannot make new purchases or guarantees of troubled assets, but can still administer existing TARP investments and continue to expend TARP funds previously obligated. SIGTARP has an unwavering commitment to protect taxpayers who funded TARP. SIGTARP has conducted oversight of TARP funds and has promoted transparency related to TARP through 14 quarterly reports to Congress and 17 published audits and evaluations as of March 31, 2012. As of that date, SIGTARP had issued 96 recommendations designed to improve TARP programs and make them less susceptible to fraud, waste, and abuse.

SIGTARP has aggressively uncovered and stopped fraud related to TARP, with investigations resulting in criminal convictions of 50 defendants, of whom 23 have been sentenced to prison as of April 12, 2012, with others awaiting sentencing. We are not slowing down, and under the authorizing provisions of EESA, SIGTARP will remain on watch as long as Treasury holds an investment or guarantee under TARP.

Role in Financial Oversight

SIGTARP is committed to vigorous oversight of TARP's unprecedented commitment of billions of taxpayer dollars. SIGTARP's goal is to promote economic stability by assiduously protecting the interests of those who fund the TARP programs -- i.e., the American taxpayers. SIGTARP fulfills its oversight role on multiple parallel tracks: auditing various aspects of TARP-related programs and activities; investigating allegations of fraud, waste, and abuse related to TARP programs; coordinating closely with other oversight bodies; and striving to promote transparency in TARP programs.

Fraud related to bailout funds has become the "next wave of financial fraud cases" as predicted by FBI Director Robert Mueller, and SIGTARP is making a difference in policing this fraud with criminal charges against 78 individuals as of April 12, 2012. SIGTARP has uncovered fraud that led to the collapse of institutions and involved deception and greed by key insiders that pre-dated TARP and contributed to the financial crisis. Financial fraud that leads to the downfall of an institution wreaks havoc on communities. People who worked hard and played by the rules can no longer obtain loans for homes, education, or small businesses. Employees of the institution lose their jobs and investors are often wiped out. SIGTARP and its law enforcement partners are ensuring that justice is served. SIGTARP actively supports the prosecution of individuals it investigates. Of the 78 individuals charged, 50 have been criminally convicted. Those convicted face serious time in prison with 23 of these individuals sentenced to prison as of April 12, 2012. The most significant prosecution to date arising out of the financial crisis resulted in a prison sentence of 30 years for Lee Farkas, former chairman of Taylor, Bean & Whitaker ("TBW"); prison sentences ranging from 3 months to 8 years for six co-conspirators at TBW and TARP-approved Colonial Bank, with one more recently convicted co-conspirator awaiting sentencing; and court-ordered restitution of $3.5 billion, for an eight-year $2.9 billion fraud scheme that led to the failure of TBW and Colonial.

SIGTARP's investigations have resulted in orders of restitution of $3.6 billion and orders of forfeiture of $126.8 million. While the ultimate recovery remains to be seen, SIGTARP has already assisted in the recovery of $151.5 million. SIGTARP also prevented $553 million in TARP funds from going out to Colonial Bank. With more than 150 ongoing investigations, SIGTARP is committed to stopping fraud, deterring criminal behavior, and bringing criminals to justice.

Recent, Current or Ongoing Work in Financial Oversight

Community Banks

Smaller and medium size banks are not exiting TARP with the same speed as the larger banks, with 434 financial institutions still in TARP as of March 31, 2012. Of these, many are not paying their TARP dividend and in some cases, the banks are operating under an order by their regulator. Compared with larger banks, community banks may face an uphill battle to exit TARP. Community banks do not have the same access to capital as the larger banks. They are more exposed to distressed commercial real estate related assets and non-performing loans.

Despite dramatic efforts to expedite the exit of the largest banks from TARP, there appears to be no corresponding concrete plan for community banks' exit from TARP. The only exit strategy for smaller TARP banks that has been announced was the Small Business Lending Fund ("SBLF"). Through this program, Treasury invested $4 billion in smaller banks. However, more than half of those dollars (approximately $2.2 billion) went to swapping 137 TARP banks out of TARP's Capital Purchase Program ("CPP") and into this non-TARP Government program. This program ties increased lending to a dividend rate that is less than the TARP 5% dividend rate, but removes executive compensation restrictions and any perceived TARP stigma, the two complaints SIGTARP heard from some of the largest banks. Banks that were not paying their TARP dividend were not eligible to apply for SBLF. However, 320 of the more than 525 banks left in TARP before SBLF's June 2011 application deadline applied to swap into SBLF. For these banks, SBLF may have been their TARP exit plan.

Community banks need a clear exit path out of TARP that is put into action well before a scheduled rise in the TARP dividend (beginning in the fall of 2013 for many banks) from 5% to 9%. The best exit path for community banks should involve access to new capital to replace the TARP capital. SIGTARP is concerned that when the dividend rate increases, many of these banks will remain in TARP but still be unable to access new capital. If that is the case, many will have no means either to exit TARP or to pay their required dividend payments.

Owing to the number of small and medium-size banks that continue to experience high losses and financial difficulties, and in order to prevent a total TARP loss, Treasury has agreed on a case-by-case basis to an increasing number of restructurings, exchanges, and sales of the TARP investments, sometimes at a steep discount. Because Treasury has shown a willingness to enter into these transactions, community banks may be relying on Treasury to enter into a similar transaction with them prior to the dividend rise. This impression could create moral hazard concerns by taking away incentives for banks to find capital on their own – a necessary step to exit TARP.

Treasury should commit to prudent stewardship of its TARP investments and take immediate action to ensure that as many banks as possible repay taxpayers and to prepare to deal with the banks that cannot. SIGTARP recommended that Treasury assess whether it should renegotiate the terms of its CPP contracts for those community banks that will not be able to exit TARP prior to the dividend rate increase. All banks, regardless of their size, received CPP funds on the same terms, but the one-size-fits-all repayment terms may not fit all. If many of these banks are not paying the 5% dividends, an increase to 9% may not have the intended effect of incentivizing them to exit TARP if they have no ability to raise capital. It may have the opposite effect as many of these banks will scramble to raise capital in the markets at the same time, at potentially less than favorable terms, which could flood the markets and have a destabilizing effect on communities. The banks may put enormous pressure on Treasury to agree to restructure or sell (at a steep discount) its investments in hundreds of banks during the same time period because Treasury may have no other choice other than face a complete loss. This could put the taxpayers' investment in these banks in jeopardy.

Recommendations to Treasury on Community Banks

In October 2011, SIGTARP made two recommendations to Treasury in regard to community banks in CPP:[1]

- Treasury, in consultation with Federal banking regulators, should develop a clear TARP exit path to ensure that as many community banks as possible repay the TARP investment and prepare to deal with the banks that cannot. Treasury should develop criteria pertaining to restructurings, exchanges, and sales of its TARP investments (including any discount of the TARP investment, the treatment of unpaid TARP dividend and interest payments, and warrants).

- Treasury should assess whether it should renegotiate the terms of its Capital Purchase Program contracts for those community banks that will not be able to exit TARP prior to the dividend rate increase in order to help preserve the value of taxpayers' investments.

In response, Treasury entered into a financial agency agreement with Houlihan Lokey Capital, Inc. ("Houlihan Lokey") for capital markets disposition services for its remaining CPP investments. Under the terms of the November 29, 2011, agreement, Treasury will pay Houlihan Lokey a flat fee of $375,000 per month for a term of 12 months, for a total of $4.5 million for the year, with the option to extend the term of the agreement for an additional six months. Treasury stated that Houlihan Lokey will act as Treasury's transaction structuring agent to perform services relating to the disposition of CPP investments, including:

- "Analyzing, reviewing and documenting financial, business, regulatory, and market information related to potential transactions of CPP investments;

- "Advising and monitoring restructuring strategies prior to the disposition of CPP investments;

(Endnotes)

1   SIGTARP, "Quarterly Report to Congress," October 27, 2011, *www.sigtarp.gov/reports/congress/2011/October2011_Quarterly_Report_to_Congress.pdf*

Appendix A:
Audit of the Financial Stability Oversight Council's Controls over Non-public Information

Report to the Financial Stability Oversight Council and the Congress

---

Prepared by The Council of Inspectors General on Financial Oversight

June 2012

Abbreviations and Acronyms

Bylaws	Rules of Organization of the Financial Stability Oversight Council
CIDI	Covered Insured Depository Institution
CIGFO	Council of Inspectors General on Financial Oversight
Dodd-Frank Act	Dodd-Frank Wall Street Reform and Consumer Protection Act
FFIEC	Federal Financial Institutions Examination Council
FISMA	Federal Information Security Management Act
FSOC or Council	Financial Stability Oversight Council
MOU	Memorandum of Understanding Regarding the Treatment of Non-public Information Shared Among Parties Pursuant to the Dodd-Frank Wall Street Reform and Consumer Protection Act
NIST	National Institute of Standards and Technology
OFR	Office of Financial Research
OIG	Office of Inspector General
Transparency Policy	Transparency Policy for the Financial Stability Oversight Council
Treasury	Department of the Treasury

DEPARTMENT OF THE TREASURY
WASHINGTON, D.C. 20220

June 22, 2012

The Honorable Timothy Geithner
Chair, Financial Stability Oversight Council
Washington D.C. 20220

Dear Mr. Chairman:

I am pleased to present to you a copy of the first Council of Inspectors General on Financial Oversight (CIGFO) report titled, *Audit of the Financial Stability Oversight Council's Controls over Non-public Information.*

Given the importance of protecting Financial Stability Oversight Council (FSOC) information, on December 8, 2011 Jon Rymer, Inspector General, Federal Deposit Insurance Corporation, and Vice Chair, CIGFO, proposed convening a working group to examine FSOC's controls for ensuring that its non-public information is properly safeguarded from unauthorized disclosure. The proposal was approved, and a CIGFO Working Group completed a review.

This CIGFO report encourages FSOC to continue its ongoing efforts, further examine the issues raised in our report with respect to information control differences, and prepare for possible security upgrades as economic conditions change and new threats to the stability of the United States financial system emerge.

I would like to take this opportunity to thank the Working Group members responsible for this report, each of whom is listed in Appendix III. In addition, I appreciate the support of the FSOC Member agencies' staff as well, especially those Treasury officials who assisted with this effort.

The CIGFO looks forward to working with you on this and other issues. In accordance with the Dodd-Frank Act, CIGFO is providing this report to the Congress.

Sincerely,

Eric M. Thorson
Chair
Council of Inspectors General
on Financial Oversight

Enclosure(s)

Executive Summary

Why and How We Conducted the Review

The landmark Dodd-Frank Wall Street Reform and Consumer Protection Act (Dodd-Frank Act) created a comprehensive new regulatory and resolution framework designed to avoid the severe consequences of financial instability. The Dodd-Frank Act created, among other things, the Council of Inspectors General on Financial Oversight (CIGFO). One of CIGFO's statutory functions is to provide oversight of the Financial Stability Oversight Council (FSOC or Council). Specifically, the law grants CIGFO the authority to convene a working group, by a majority vote, for the purpose of evaluating the effectiveness and internal operations of FSOC.

FSOC is charged with identifying risks to the nation's financial stability, promoting market discipline, and responding to emerging threats to the stability of the nation's financial system. These responsibilities are significant, and any decisions coming from FSOC could impact the U.S. financial system and have repercussions for global financial institutions and systems. The information that FSOC collects, deliberations it has, and decisions it implements must be managed and controlled.

FSOC is chaired by the Secretary of the Treasury. Within the Department of the Treasury (Treasury), a dedicated policy office, led by a Deputy Assistant Secretary, functions as the FSOC Secretariat and serves as a mechanism to bring issues to the Council quickly through a coordinated process. The 10 voting members of FSOC provide a federal regulatory perspective and an independent insurance expert's view. The five nonvoting members offer different insights as state-level representatives from bank, securities, and insurance regulators or as the directors of the new offices within Treasury established by the Dodd-Frank Act – the Office of Financial Research (OFR) and the Federal Insurance Office.

On December 8, 2011, Jon Rymer, Inspector General, Federal Deposit Insurance Corporation, and Vice Chair, CIGFO, proposed convening a working group to examine FSOC's controls and protocols for ensuring that its non-public information, deliberations, and decisions are properly safeguarded from unauthorized disclosure. The proposal was approved and the CIGFO Working Group was formed.

To accomplish its objective, the CIGFO Working Group identified the controls and protocols in place at each of the FSOC federal agency members to safeguard FSOC information and the manner in which FSOC as a whole safeguards information from unauthorized disclosure. The audit was intended to capture the current information exchange environment as well as identify any potential risk or gaps in controls over information exchange and bring those issues to the attention of FSOC as it continues to carry out its mission. We did not include the FSOC independent and state members in this review.

What We Learned

FSOC understands that its ability to safely share information among its members is critical to its effectiveness. To date, a limited amount of non-public information, primarily information related to rulemakings, meetings, and other routine activities, has been exchanged among Council members.

Joint work among FSOC members to identify and mitigate risks to financial stability has begun, and data sharing will expand as OFR continues to build its capacity. To protect the exchange of information, the Council members entered into a memorandum of understanding governing the treatment of non-public information that relies on each agency to use the controls in place at their respective agencies.

All FSOC federal agency members are subject to the Federal Information Security Management Act (FISMA), which requires that federal agencies review their information and determine appropriate security controls over that information commensurate with risk. We did, however, identify differences in how FSOC federal agency members mark non-public information as well as differences for handling non-public information. Without addressing these differences, there is a risk that senders and receivers of FSOC non-public information may not apply a consistent level of controls. In this regard, it is important to note that FSOC has begun to address these differences among its members through a March 2012 project that is being coordinated by the FSOC Data Committee. FSOC has requested detailed information gathered during our review to assist with this project.

In preparation for the increase in new types of non-public information under the Dodd-Frank Act and mindful of its duty to safely share that information among its members, we learned that the FSOC Secretariat is developing, with OFR, two tools to support secure collaboration. As FSOC continues to develop those tools for information sharing, it should consider that some of the new information developed under the Dodd-Frank Act as well as unexpected economic events may require controls greater than those currently in place or being planned among Council members. Similarly, appropriate safeguards will need to be considered and possibly upgraded by each FSOC federal agency member to ensure timely and secure access to the information. In the interim, FSOC should consider having a contingency plan in place to quickly and safely exchange information under a crisis environment. Such a plan should also contemplate FSOC's independent and state members.

Conclusion and Matters for Consideration

We acknowledge that FSOC is still evolving and a number of information-sharing projects are under development. For this reason, we are not making recommendations at this time. However, we encourage the Council to continue ongoing efforts, further examine the issues raised in our report with respect to commonalities and differences of member agencies, and prepare for possible security upgrades for information that may need to be exchanged as economic conditions change and new threats to the stability of the U.S. financial system emerge. We underscore the importance of acting in a timely manner.

FSOC Comments

On June 12, 2012, we received comments on our draft report from the Treasury Acting General Counsel on behalf of FSOC. (See Appendix II.) The Acting General Counsel's comments acknowledged the observations and suggestions we made. His response indicates that in the event any new data is designated "high impact," meaning the release of such data could result in catastrophic adverse impact on the financial system, FSOC members and member agencies would review how to address issues associated with safeguards and protocols to accommodate the exchange of such data. We would reiterate the value of preparing for that possibility.

Results of CIGFO Working Group Review

Introduction

CIGFO is pleased to report the results of its audit of the controls that FSOC has in place to protect non-public information from unauthorized disclosure. This is the first report that a CIGFO Working Group has issued to the Council and the Congress as part of CIGFO's authority to oversee FSOC under the Dodd-Frank Act.

In light of the sensitive nature of the information that could emerge and be shared as FSOC members carry out their new mandate under the Dodd-Frank Act, CIGFO identified information security controls as an area where the Inspectors General could bring their collective expertise to bear. Thus, CIGFO undertook a review to provide a snapshot of the current information control environment at the individual federal agency member level, determine any related initiatives the federal agency members and FSOC were undertaking, and then identify potential risks or gaps that FSOC as a whole may wish to consider as it continues to evolve the control framework that will govern the exchange of information between and among its various members.

In presenting these results, we are mindful that FSOC is a new entity and has not yet exchanged large amounts of non-public information, nor has it needed to confront the type of precipitous economic distress that prompted the recent financial crisis. However, FSOC and its members need to be well positioned to address threats to the stability of the financial system. Protecting the sensitive information that they possess, exchange, and discuss as they address these threats – both as individual members and as a collective Council – is of paramount importance.

To provide context for the report, we first present background information on FSOC, its membership, and its governance structure. Next, we discuss the FSOC information control environment, including commonalities and differences among FSOC federal agency members, ongoing initiatives to safely share information, and additional controls that may be needed going forward. Finally, we provide our concluding thoughts and matters for FSOC to consider.

Appendix I presents our audit objective and approach in more detail. Appendix II includes FSOC's comments on a draft of this report. Appendix III provides a listing of the CIGFO Working Group participants.

Background

FSOC was established to create joint accountability for identifying and mitigating potential threats to the stability of the nation's financial system. By creating FSOC, Congress recognized that financial stability would require the collective engagement of the entire financial regulatory community.

FSOC consists of 10 voting members and 5 nonvoting members and brings together the expertise of federal financial regulators, state regulators, and an insurance expert appointed by the President with Senate confirmation. FSOC is an important new function designed to fill the gaps in regulatory oversight. For the first time, a single entity has the collective accountability for identifying and limiting risks to the financial system as a whole. Each FSOC member comes to the table with unique and diverse responsibilities, interests, and expertise. Some member agencies have existed for a long time, while others are newly created.

Table 1: FSOC's Primary Purpose
• Identify risks to the financial stability of the U.S. that could arise from the material financial distress or failure, or ongoing activities, of large, interconnected bank holding companies or nonbank financial companies, or that could arise outside the financial services marketplace.
• Promote market discipline, by eliminating expectations on the part of shareholders, creditors, and counterparties of such companies that the U.S. government will shield them from losses in the event of failure.
• Respond to emerging threats to the stability of the U.S. financial system.

Table 2: FSOC Membership	
Federal Agency Members	**Independent and State Members**
• Secretary of the Treasury, Chairperson (v)	• Independent member with insurance expertise (v)
• Chairman of the Board of Governors of the Federal Reserve System (v)	• State Insurance Commissioner
• Comptroller of the Currency (v)	• State Banking Supervisor
• Director of the Bureau of Consumer Financial Protection (v)	• State Securities Commissioner
• Chairman of the Securities and Exchange Commission (v)	
• Chairperson of the Federal Deposit Insurance Corporation (v)	
• Chairperson of the Commodity Futures Trading Commission (v)	
• Director of the Federal Housing Finance Agency (v)	
• Chairman of the National Credit Union Administration Board (v)	
• Director of the Office of Financial Research	
• Director of the Federal Insurance Office	

Source: 12 U.S.C. 5321(b)   (v) Indicates Voting Member

FSOC is chaired by the Secretary of the Treasury. Within Treasury, a dedicated policy office, led by a Deputy Assistant Secretary, functions as the FSOC Secretariat and serves as a mechanism to bring issues to the Council quickly through a coordinated process. Voting members of FSOC provide a federal regulatory perspective and an independent insurance expert's view. The nonvoting members offer different insights as state-level representatives from bank, securities, and insurance regulators or as the directors of the new offices within the Treasury established by the Dodd-Frank Act – OFR and the Federal Insurance Office.

To carry out its mission, FSOC employs a committee structure.[15] Individual committees handle key responsibilities and require significant sharing of information to fully understand the complex issues at hand. The FSOC Data Committee, for example, supports coordination of, and consultation on, agency rulemakings on data collection, and seeks to minimize duplication of data gathering operations. This committee supports a coordinated approach to information sharing and provides direction to, and requests data from, OFR. Additionally, the committee works with OFR on data standardization.

OFR is the research arm of FSOC. As outlined in the Dodd-Frank Act, OFR supports the Council and member agencies by collecting and disseminating data to the Council and member agencies; standardizing the types and formats of data reported and collected; performing research; developing tools for risk measurement and monitoring; making the results of OFR's activities available to financial regulatory agencies; and assisting member agencies in determining the types and formats of data authorized under the Dodd-Frank Act to be collected by the member agencies.

Approach

The objective of our audit was to examine the controls and protocols that FSOC and its federal agency members employ to safeguard non-public information collected by, and exchanged with, FSOC members from unauthorized disclosure. We did not assess whether controls in place were effective or commensurate with risk, determine whether FSOC federal agency members were complying with controls, or evaluate controls and protocols of the FSOC independent and state members. We conducted our work from February through May 2012 in accordance with generally accepted government auditing standards.

As members of the CIGFO Working Group, each Office of Inspector General (OIG) conducted a survey of its FSOC federal agency member(s) to obtain information regarding the current status of each member's existing policies, procedures, and practices related to securing non-public FSOC information. The information was gathered through the use of a CIGFO Working Group-developed questionnaire based on information security control concepts in FISMA.

Each agency's OIG presented its specific findings to its respective agency management who were given the opportunity to provide additional comments. The results from each OIG and the FSOC Secretariat were reviewed to identify current controls as well as opportunities to strengthen overall controls over non-public FSOC information. We provided a briefing on the overall results of our work to FSOC and OFR staff on April 27, 2012.

---

15 FSOC's committee structure consists of the Deputies Committee and the Systemic Risk Committee. The Systemic Risk Committee has two sub-committees – the Institutions Sub-committee and the Markets Sub-committee. There are also five Standing Functional Committees – Designations of Nonbank Financial Companies; Designations of Financial Market Utilities and Payment, Clearing, and Settlement Activities; Heightened Prudential Standards; Orderly Liquidation Authority, Resolution Plans; and Data.

The Current FSOC Information Exchange Control Environment

Information collection, analysis, exchange, and deliberation are critical components of FSOC activity. Unauthorized disclosure of non-public information, in particular, is a risk that FSOC faces as it carries out its responsibilities under the Dodd-Frank Act. To date, exchange of information has been limited primarily to that associated with rulemakings and communications during meetings; however, the volume and nature of information exchanged could change substantially in the future. In the next sections of this report, we describe, at a high level, the internal information security control environments of FSOC federal agency members and how related security controls come into play when non-public information is exchanged beyond the members' control environment.

FSOC Memorandum of Understanding Governs Information Exchange

FSOC members have a statutory obligation to maintain the confidentiality of any data, information, and reports submitted under the Dodd-Frank Act. FSOC incorporated much of that confidentiality requirement into its governance documents, including in the *Rules of Organization of the Financial Stability Oversight Council* (known as the Bylaws) as well as the *Transparency Policy for the Financial Stability Oversight Council* (Transparency Policy). The Bylaws specifically require that FSOC members protect and maintain the confidentiality of any data, information, and reports submitted or available to them. The Transparency Policy governs FSOC meetings and requires the protection of information in order to prevent destabilizing market speculation that could occur if confidential information were to be disclosed.

The Bylaws also provide that FSOC members may enter into a memorandum of understanding regarding the treatment of confidential information. In this regard, all FSOC members signed the *Memorandum of Understanding Regarding the Treatment of Non-public Information Shared Among Parties Pursuant to the Dodd-Frank Wall Street Reform and Consumer Protection Act* (MOU), which sets forth the understanding of all FSOC members regarding the treatment of non-public information. The MOU, with an effective date of April 15, 2011, is the foundation for the secure exchange of non-public FSOC information.

The MOU defines "non-public information" as any data, information, or reports submitted, received, or shared among FSOC members in connection with or related to the functions and activities of FSOC or OFR. Non-public information includes the information itself, in any form, including oral communication, and any document to the extent it contains such information. The MOU presumes that non-public information exchanged under its terms is confidential.

According to the MOU, each FSOC member "will take all steps reasonably necessary to preserve, protect and maintain all privileges and claims of confidentiality." In effect, the MOU relies on the controls of each FSOC member to safeguard non-public FSOC information. The premise underlying that requirement is that all FSOC members know what steps are, in fact, reasonably necessary to safeguard FSOC non-public information both internally and when exchanging non-public information among FSOC's membership.

FSOC Federal Agency Members Use a Common Information Security Framework

An important commonality among FSOC federal agency members is that each member is subject to FISMA. FISMA tasked the National Institute of Standards and Technology (NIST) with various responsibilities, including, among other things, the development of information security standards to be used by federal agencies to categorize information and information systems collected or maintained by or on behalf of each agency. The objective of such categorization is to provide appropriate levels of information security according to a range of impact levels.

NIST Federal Information Processing Standard 199[16] requires that federal agencies assess the potential impact on an organization should certain events – in this case the release of information to the public – occur. Such a release would jeopardize the information and information systems needed by the organization to accomplish its assigned

Table 3: Impact-Level Designations
• Low – Limited adverse impact.
• Moderate – Serious adverse impact.
• High – Severe or catastrophic adverse impact.

Source: Federal Information Processing Standard 199

mission, protect its assets, fulfill its legal responsibilities, maintain its day-to-day functions, and protect individuals. NIST establishes three levels of potential impact – "low," "moderate," or "high"– as defined in Table 3. The standards primarily relate to information system controls.

During our review, we determined that all FSOC federal agency members are subject to FISMA. Further, all FSOC federal agency members currently handle information designated at a "moderate" impact level.

NIST standards and guidelines require that federal agencies implement baseline controls for their systems commensurate with their impact-level designations. Those standards and guidelines allow agencies flexibility to determine how to implement controls and provide agencies with the ability to implement controls that are greater than baseline requirements. As a result, controls in place at one federal agency may not be commensurate with controls in place at another federal agency even though the agencies' impact-level designations may be the same. As discussed later in this report, we found that there were control differences among FSOC federal agency members.

FISMA requires that the agency that owns or is the steward of information is responsible for ensuring that proper security controls govern that information even when it is transferred to another agency. Additionally, automated systems that house information at various impact-level designations must set controls at the greatest of those impact levels. Finally, FISMA along with OMB policy lays out a framework for annual information technology security reviews, reporting, and remediation planning.[17]

Agency FISMA reports and related OIG evaluations describe the strengths and weaknesses of the information security controls within each FSOC federal agency member. This report focuses on security controls impacting the exchange of information from one FSOC federal agency member to another, as those controls are most relevant to the Council.

---

16   Federal Information Processing Standard 199, *Standards for Security Categorization of Federal Information and Information Systems* (Feb. 2004).

17   OMB Circular No. A-130, Management of Federal Information Resources; and annual FISMA reporting instructions.

Differences in FSOC Federal Agency Member Controls

As discussed below, we identified differences in how FSOC federal agency members mark non-public information as well as differences in controls over the handling of non-public information. Those differences reduce the assurance that FSOC federal agency members receiving information will apply the same level of security controls as those sending the information.

FSOC Federal Agency Members Have Different Markings for Non-public Information

We found that FSOC federal agency members use different markings to identify non-public information, and those markings signify specific control requirements. Marking refers to the process of labeling hardcopy or electronic information as non-public information. Table 4 summarizes the seven different marking types we found during our work.

Without a common marking vocabulary and understanding of what each marking implies, it is difficult for FSOC federal agency members to know the appropriate controls to apply to information shared with other FSOC members. For example, is a "sensitive" marking for one agency's information the same as a "predecisional" marking for another agency's information, and do the same information security controls apply? As previously mentioned, the MOU requires that each agency take steps reasonably necessary to safeguard non-public information.

While our work did not expressly cover FSOC independent and state members, we understand that these members have received non-public information. Therefore, our concern with information marking goes beyond FSOC federal agency members and could affect the sharing of information among other members. This concern is heightened because the FSOC independent and state members may change at 6- and 2-year intervals, respectively, and the continuity of established safeguards is uncertain.

We note that the issue of how federal agencies mark non-public information and the controls commensurate with those markings is a government-wide concern.

Table 4: FSOC Federal Agency Member Markings
• Confidential
• Sensitive But Unclassified
• Controlled Unclassified
• Sensitive
• Business Sensitive
• Restricted
• Predecisional

Source: CIGFO Working Group Analysis

The President signed Executive Order 13556, *Controlled Unclassified Information*, on November 4, 2010, to address the ad hoc, agency-specific policies, procedures, and markings for safeguarding and controlling information. The Executive Order notes that this inefficient, confusing patchwork has resulted in inconsistent marking and safeguarding of documents, led to unclear or unnecessarily restrictive dissemination policies, and created impediments to authorized information sharing. According to the Executive Order, the National Archives and Records Administration is responsible for implementing the order and overseeing agency actions. Those efforts are underway, but the program is not yet complete. In the interim, FSOC should determine how to bridge the gap of information marking and corresponding controls.

Some FSOC federal agency members who routinely share information among one another have arrangements in place to bridge this marking gap that pre-date the Dodd-Frank Act. For example, the Federal Financial Institutions Examination Council (FFIEC), whose membership includes the Board of Governors of the Federal Reserve System, the Federal Deposit Insurance Corporation, the National Credit Union Administration, and the Office of the Comptroller of the Currency, has a Task Force on Information Sharing that promotes the sharing of electronic information among FFIEC agencies. The task force provides a forum for FFIEC members to discuss and address issues affecting the quality, consistency, efficiency, and security of interagency information sharing. Additionally, some FSOC federal agency members have their own information-sharing agreements in place with other federal agencies.

During our review, we learned that, as of March 8, 2012, the FSOC Data Committee is coordinating a project to establish an FSOC-wide framework for classifying, marking, and handling data. We understand that OFR expects to develop and share its own initial classification structure during fiscal year 2012 and will then work with Council members to either develop a common classification structure or a mapping among dissimilar classification structures in fiscal year 2013. Further, the FSOC Data Committee is reviewing information-sharing processes in place at the FFIEC.

FSOC Federal Agency Members Have Different Controls for Handling Non-public Information

FSOC federal agency members have different policies and procedures governing the handling of non-public information. Our survey included a number of questions concerning policies, procedures, and protocols over personnel who handle non-public information. We found that FSOC federal agency members fall along a continuum, with some members having robust policies and procedures over information handling while others had few policies and procedures. This continuum reflects an overall control environment with varying levels of safeguards to be used by all parties involved in the process of sharing FSOC information.

Table 5 indentifies the six most common control differences that we identified during our work. As an example, some agencies did not have explicit policies and procedures governing oral communication of non-public information, while others had specific protocols such as prohibiting discussion of non-public information while on cell phones. As other examples, although all FSOC federal agency members are subject to the Office of Government Ethics Standards of Ethical Conduct,[18] some agencies have adopted supplemental standards prohibiting the purchase and sale of securities by the employee

Table 5: Federal Agency Member Control Differences for Handling Non-public Information

- Oral communication
- Supplemental prohibition on financial interest
- Contractor confidentiality and nondisclosure
- Encryption
- Meeting-related controls
- Protocols to track information exchange

Source: CIGFO Working Group Analysis

---

18   5 C.F.R. Part 2635.

and the employee's family when the employee is in possession of material non-public information. Some FSOC federal agency members had specific policies and procedures on when to encrypt non-public information, but others did not. Finally, one FSOC federal agency member is initiating a formal information-sharing protocol between the agency, FSOC, and OFR to track both information sent from the agency as well as to the agency, but most FSOC federal agency members do not have such protocols in place.

During our April 27, 2012, briefing to the FSOC Secretariat and OFR staff on the results of our review, staff requested that we provide more detail on policies and procedures covering information marking and handling. Staff stated that doing so would help FSOC's review of information-sharing protocols. We agreed to provide that information.

FSOC Information Exchange Efforts Should Consider Existing Member Control Differences and Potential Vulnerabilities

Joint work among FSOC members to identify and mitigate risks to financial stability has begun, and data sharing will expand as the OFR continues to build its capacity to gather information and perform analysis. That analysis includes the development of new information not previously held by or exchanged among Council members, including, among other things, information pertaining to threats to the U.S. financial system. A greater volume of this new information is anticipated in the near future, beginning with the July 1, 2012, deadline for the submission of resolution plans (known as living wills)[19] for certain institutions with $250 billion or more in total assets.

In preparation for the increase in new types of non-public information and mindful of its duty to safely share that information among its members, the FSOC Secretariat informed us that it is developing, with OFR, two tools to support secure collaboration. Based on descriptions provided by the FSOC Secretariat, the tools, which are in different stages of development, include (1) a data transmission protocol currently used by other Council members that will enable interagency data set exchange and (2) a secure collaboration tool for sharing documents. The secure collaboration tool will first be used between the FSOC Secretariat and OFR before access is provided to other Council members. The collaboration tool will reside within Treasury and access will be granted to Council members by Treasury. In addition, OFR has established a short-term analytical environment for its own researchers to use and for the FSOC Secretariat to access certain OFR datasets and related analytical tools. Whether this tool will be used to collaborate among Council members is, according to FSOC, still under review.

As the design and testing continue on these tools, FSOC and OFR need to consider the impact-level designation of the information that may be housed in those tools. As part of our review, we asked each FSOC federal agency member whether new information they would be required to develop, produce, or provide under the Dodd-Frank Act required a reassessment of their maximum impact-level designation. As discussed previously, under NIST standards, the owner or steward of information is required to make the

---

19   77 Fed. Reg. 3075 (Jan. 23, 2012). The July 1, 2012, date corresponds with Covered Insured Depository Institutions (CIDI) whose parent company, as of November 30, 2011, had $250 billion or more in total nonbank assets. Plans are due on July 1, 2013, from CIDIs whose parent company, as of November 30, 2011, had $100 billion or more in total nonbank assets and on December 31, 2013, for all other CIDIs.

decision regarding the impact-level designation.

Nearly all of the FSOC federal agency members indicated that their existing "moderate" impact level was appropriate for their respective new Dodd-Frank Act information; however, one agency indicated that under certain economic circumstances, information it could provide to FSOC may be considered to be at the "high" impact level. The FSOC Secretariat, OFR, and Federal Insurance Office all reported that they could not rule out the possibility that new information they develop in the future under the Dodd-Frank Act would require adjustment to existing security levels. NIST defines a "moderate" impact-level designation as one in which the disclosure, modification, destruction, or disruption of access to that information would have a serious adverse effect on the agency's operations, assets or personnel. A "high" impact-level designation is one in which the disclosure, modification, destruction, or disruption of access to that information would have a severe or catastrophic adverse effect on the agency's operations, assets or personnel.[20]

Given this uncertainty and the possibility that any Council member could make a future determination that some of its information is at the "high" impact level, appropriate safeguards will need to be considered and possibly upgraded by each FSOC federal agency member for exchanging FSOC information. For example, if FSOC federal agency members have access to Treasury tools and have rights to download information onto their own servers or individual computers and print and store information, specific controls would need to be in place at the FSOC federal agency member beyond the controls used by the Treasury to grant remote access. We understand from our interviews that there are potential costs – depending on how such information could be exchanged – involved in upgrading controls for FSOC federal agency members who may receive "high" impact-level information. We were advised that FSOC intends to minimize the cost burden for its members as it continues to develop information-sharing tools. In addition, FSOC federal agency members would require lead time to put those additional controls in place before the exchange of information. The issue of lead time involved could take on greater importance, should, as indicated by one FSOC federal agency member, unexpected economic events make certain FSOC information "high" impact and require information be exchanged among FSOC members without time to ensure proper controls are in place.

As FSOC continues to consider its information-sharing protocols, it should factor in the potential for "high" impact-level information as well as the differences in information controls among its members. In the interim, FSOC should consider having a contingency plan in place to quickly exchange "high" impact-level information under a crisis environment.

---

20   Federal Information Processing Standards Publication 199. NIST amplifies that severe or catastrophic adverse effect means a severe degradation in or loss of mission capability to an extent and duration that the organization is not able to perform one or more of its primary functions; results in major damage to organization assets; results in major financial loss; or severe or catastrophic harm to individuals involving loss of life or serious life-threatening injuries.

Conclusion and Matters for Consideration

Given the volatility of the ever-changing economic conditions and the potential threats to the financial stability of the U.S. in a global environment, FSOC members must be ready to act quickly in carrying out their mission under the Dodd-Frank Act. We acknowledge that the Council is still evolving and a number of information-sharing projects are under development. With that in mind, we are not making recommendations at this time. However, we encourage the members of the Council, in the spirit of the MOU, to continue the ongoing efforts to protect the non-public information that they currently possess and will develop over time.

We also believe that FSOC would be well-served to further examine the issues raised in this report to increase their understanding of the differences in members' information control environments and determine whether those differences pose a risk of unauthorized disclosure of a magnitude that the Council would need to address on an FSOC-wide basis. Additionally, in examining differences, some best practices could emerge to the benefit of the Council as a whole. To that end, as requested, we are providing the FSOC Secretariat with a more detailed summary of the work of the individual OIGs involved in our CIGFO Working Group.

Finally, with particular regard to the tools under development for secure collaboration and controlled access to data shared among FSOC members, we underscore the importance of acting in a timely manner to complete the initiatives, considering the potential heightened impact designation of new information and the control ramifications of decisions made about such information. Taken together, such actions will help to ensure the readiness of FSOC members to keep pace with and react quickly to any threats to financial stability, knowing that all information possessed and exchanged as part of those efforts is protected as appropriate.

Summary of FSOC Comments

On June 12, 2012, we received comments on our draft report from the Treasury Acting General Counsel on behalf of FSOC. These comments are included in their entirety in Appendix II. The Acting General Counsel acknowledged the observations and suggestions we made. His response references the MOU that FSOC put in place to establish protocols for protecting the confidentiality of non-public information and the Bylaws that contain a provision related to protecting such information. The Data Committee's ongoing efforts to align FSOC members' protocols for classifying, marking, and handling data are mentioned. His response also affirms that the offices and staff of the Department of the Treasury engaged in FSOC work, along with the independent member with insurance expertise and his staff, operate within Treasury's information security infrastructure.

Finally, the Acting General Counsel's response indicates that in the event any new data is designated "high impact," meaning the release of such data could result in catastrophic adverse impact on the financial system, FSOC members and member agencies would review how to address issues associated with safeguards and protocols to accommodate the exchange of such data. We would reiterate the value of preparing for that possibility.

APPENDIX I: Objective, Scope, and Methodology

Objective

The audit objective was to examine the controls and protocols that FSOC and its federal agency members employ to safeguard non-public information collected by, and exchanged with, FSOC federal agency members from unauthorized disclosure. We did not assess whether controls in place were effective or commensurate with risk, determine whether FSOC federal agency members were complying with controls, or include the FSOC independent and state members in the review.

We conducted our performance audit work from February through May 2012 in accordance with generally accepted government auditing standards applicable to the objective and scope of the survey defined in the February 2012 CIGFO Survey Program. Those standards require that we plan and perform the audit to obtain sufficient, appropriate evidence to provide a reasonable basis for our findings and conclusions based on our audit objective. We believe that the evidence obtained provides a reasonable basis for our findings and conclusions based on our audit objective. Consistent with standards and as called for in the survey program, we obtained and incorporated the views of responsible agency officials into the results of our work.

We also performed appropriate quality control procedures, such as indexing and referencing, consistent with each OIG's internal policies and procedures to ensure the reliability of our results.

Scope and Methodology

The scope of this audit included a survey of the controls and protocols the FSOC federal agency members employ to safeguard non-public information collected by, and exchanged with, FSOC members from unauthorized disclosure.

We conducted a survey of the FSOC federal agency members, including the Consumer Financial Protection Bureau; Commodity Futures Trading Commission; Federal Deposit Insurance Corporation; Federal Housing Finance Agency; Federal Insurance Office; Board of Governors of the Federal Reserve System; National Credit Union Administration; Office of the Comptroller of the Currency; Office of Financial Research; Securities and Exchange Commission; and the Department of the Treasury, through each agency's OIG. The survey was designed to obtain information regarding each member's existing policies, procedures, and practices related to securing non-public FSOC information. The information was gathered through the use of a questionnaire. The questions were generally developed based on NIST Special Publication 800-53 Rev. 3, *Recommended Security Controls for Federal Information Systems and Organizations* since all federal agencies are required to follow NIST information security guidelines to meet FISMA requirements.

Each agency's OIG requested that agency management provide responses through interviews or self-reporting responses to the questionnaire. As part of the questionnaire, agencies reported the names of their policies, procedures, and practices regarding safeguarding FSOC non-public information. Each OIG reviewed the responses and requested clarification if necessary. Agency management was also given the opportunity to provide additional comments prior to submission. In preparing this report, results from all OIGs were reviewed to identify current controls and opportunities to strengthen controls over non-public FSOC information.

APPENDIX II: FSOC Response

DEPARTMENT OF THE TREASURY
WASHINGTON, D.C. 20220

June 12, 2012

The Honorable Eric M. Thorson
Chair, Council of Inspectors General
on Financial Oversight
1500 Pennsylvania Avenue, NW
Washington, D.C. 20220

Re: Response to CIGFO's Draft Audit Report: *Audit of the Financial Stability*
       Oversight Council's Controls over Non-public Information: Report to the
       Financial Stability Oversight Council and the Congress

Dear Mr. Chairman:

Thank you for the opportunity to review and respond to your draft Audit Report, *Audit of the Financial Stability Oversight Council's Controls over Non-public Information: Report to the Financial Stability Oversight Council and the Congress, dated May 31, 2012* (the Report). The Financial Stability Oversight Council (Council) and its respective members and member agencies appreciate the Council of Inspectors General on Financial Oversight (CIGFO) Working Group's review of the Council's controls and protocols for safeguarding information. This letter responds, on behalf of the Secretary of the Treasury as Chairperson of the Council, to your Report. The staffs of Council members previously provided comments and technical corrections to CIGFO staff.

The Report does not make any recommendations to the Council at this time, although it does make a number of observations and suggestions. Specifically, the Report (1) encourages the Council federal member agencies "to continue the ongoing efforts to protect the non-public information that they currently possess and will develop over time;" (2) suggests that the Council federal member agencies "further examine the issues raised in this report to increase their understanding of the differences in members' information control environments and determine whether those differences pose a risk of unauthorized disclosure of a magnitude that the Council would need to address on [a Council]-wide basis;" and (3) underscores "the importance of acting in a timely manner to complete the initiatives [under development for secure collaboration and controlled access to data shared among [Council] members]."

Safeguarding non-public information is crucial to the work of the Council. Toward that end, the Council members and member agencies entered into a Memorandum of Understanding that establishes protocols for protecting the confidentiality of "non-public information" shared among parties pursuant to the Dodd-Frank Wall Street Reform and Consumer Protection Act. The Council also has adopted in its Rules of Organization (known as the Council's Bylaws) a provision relating to the protection of confidential and other forms of non-public information. Beyond these existing protections, as the Report acknowledges, the Council Data Committee is working to further align the Council members' protocols for classifying, marking, and handling data.

The offices of the Department of the Treasury (Treasury) engaged in the Council's work – including the Federal Insurance Office, the Office of Financial Research, and the Treasury staff supporting the Council – also adhere to the security protections and compliance obligations in place at Treasury. In addition, Treasury provides administrative and infrastructure support to the Independent Member with insurance expertise and his staff of two senior advisors. As a result, the Independent Member and his staff benefit from Treasury's information technology security infrastructure.

The Report also raises the possibility that a Council member agency could generate new data that, under the National Institute of Standards and Technology classification system, would have a "high" impact-level designation – meaning release of such data could result in catastrophic adverse impact on the financial system. The Report suggests the Council federal members and member agencies may need to design additional, and potentially new, safeguards and protocols to accommodate the exchange of such data. Should such issues arise, Council members and member agencies would review how to address them.

Thank you again for your important oversight role and the observations you make in the Report. As the Report recognizes, the Council "is still evolving and a number of information-sharing projects are under development." The Council looks forward to working with you in the future.

Sincerely,

Christopher J. Meade
Acting General Counsel

Appendix III: CIGFO Working Group

Federal Deposit Insurance Corporation – Lead Agency		
Jon Rymer, Inspector General, Federal Deposit Insurance Corporation, and CIGFO Vice Chair		
Steve Beard	John Davidovich	Adriana Rojas
Arlene Boateng	Fred Gibson	Teresa Supples
Leslee Bollea	Judy Hoyle	Sharon Tushin
Danny Craven	Mark Mulholland	Peggy Wolf, Project Lead
Board of Governors of the Federal Reserve System and Consumer Financial Protection Bureau		
Tony Castaldo	Laura Shakarji	
Trevor Gaskins	Michael VanHuysen	
Charles Liuksila		
Commodity Futures Trading Commission		
Tony Baptiste	Judy Ringle	
Edward Kelley		
Department of the Treasury		
Tim Cargill	Jeff Dye	Jen Ksanznak
Theresa Cameron	Marla Freedman	Susan Marshall
Dana Duvall	Patrick Gallagher	Bob Taylor
Federal Housing Finance Agency		
Brian Baker	Brent Melson	
Andrew Gegor	Russell Rau	
National Credit Union Administration		
Charles Funderburk		
Marvin Stith		
Securities and Exchange Commission		
Kelli Brown-Barnes	Russell Moore	
Brenda Eberle		

www.ingramcontent.com/pod-product-compliance
Lightning Source LLC
Chambersburg PA
CBHW081835170526
45167CB00007B/2809